The Tactics of Change

Doing Therapy Briefly

Richard Fisch
John H. Weakland
Lynn Segal

The Tactics of Change

Doing Therapy Briefly

Jossey-Bass Publishers
San Francisco • Washington • London • 1982

THE TACTICS OF CHANGE
Doing Therapy Briefly
by Richard Fisch, John H. Weakland, and Lynn Segal

Copyright © 1982 by: Jossey-Bass Inc., Publishers
433 California Street
San Francisco, California 94104
&
Jossey-Bass Limited
28 Banner Street
London EC1Y 8QE

Library of Congress Cataloging in Publication Data

Fisch, Richard
    The tactics of change.

    Bibliography: p. 295
    Includes index.
    1. Psychotherapy, Brief. 2. Psychotherapy.
I. Weakland, John H. II. Segal, Lynn. III. Title.
[DNLM: 1. Psychotherapy, Brief. WM 420 F528t]
RC480.55.F57   616.89′14   82-15371
ISBN 0-87589-521-2   AACR2

Manufactured in the United States of America

The paper in this book meets the guidelines for
permanence and durability of the Committee on
Production Guidelines for Book Longevity of the
Council on Library Resources.

JACKET DESIGN BY WILLI BAUM

FIRST EDITION

Code 8217

The Jossey-Bass
Social and Behavioral Science Series

To the Artistry
and Craftsmanship of
MILTON H. ERICKSON, M.D.

✤ Preface ✤

This is a book primarily on how to do psychotherapy briefly, although it has wider implications for problem resolution by the deliberate promotion of change. Doing therapy briefly is not necessarily the same as doing "brief psychotherapy." This latter designation has come to mean many things. It has often come to imply shortening treatment as a necessary expedient—an expedient imposed by limitations of treatment time or treatment personnel, limitations of resources within patients thought necessary for long-term treatment (such as "the capacity for insight"), or limitations of finances to support lengthy treatment. "Brief Therapy" also is often used synonymously with "Crisis Intervention," in which brevity of treatment is considered appropriate, but only for problems of an acute and sudden nature. There, too, it is often viewed as a stop-gap measure. Correspondingly, the great bulk of the literature on brief psychotherapy is concerned with attempts to impose limits on conventional long-term treatment, principally by modifying traditional techniques in limited ways and narrowing the goals of therapy. Thus, many proponents of brief therapy, while adhering to the idea that treatment can be shorter, feel it is applicable only to certain patients or problems, and that if brief approaches fail this is because the problem requires long-term, intensive treatment.

We believe that the dichotomy between brief and long-term therapy is an illusory one and, more importantly, that it is a hindrance to the development of therapy which is both effective and efficient. We view this dichotomy as an expectable partner of attempts to shorten treatment without serious reconsideration of views about the nature of problems and their resolution. As long as contributors to brief therapy explain human problems in terms of personal and interpersonal pathology, brief therapy is likely to remain a secondary approach to the "mainstream" of treatment, long-term therapy.

The Tactics of Change is an explicit and comprehensive manual on how to do therapy effectively and efficiently. While the book is predominantly devoted to technique, the technique described rests on a conceptualization of the nature of human problems that is discontinuous with traditional models. This is, in essence, a nonpathology model that is described more fully in *Change: Principles of Problem Formation and Problem Resolution* (Watzlawick, Weakland, and Fisch, 1974). We view *Tactics* as a companion work to *Change.* Both of these works are outgrowths of more than fifteen years of clinical research at the Brief Therapy Center of the Mental Research Institute (MRI) in Palo Alto. That research, in turn, grew out of earlier work on family-interactional therapy at MRI and from considerable stimulation provided by contact with the innovative work of Milton Erickson.

The Brief Therapy project began as an investigation of treatment employing innovative techniques for change and focusing on the main presenting complaint. It evolved, unexpectedly, into a new way of looking at human problems. *Change* is an explicit statement of that view; *Tactics* is a description and illustration of the techniques stemming from that underlying rationale. Since the publication of that former work, we have been working to refine and codify our treatment approach to make it clearer and more readily transmissible to other interested professionals.

While we view this work as a companion to *Change*, we are aware that any work must stand on its own merits. Thus, we have started the book with a concise statement of our theoretical perspective, since we repeatedly stress the relation between technique and theory. Thus, in Chapter One we present a concise statement of our premises and assumptions. In order to make the theoretical underpinnings of our approach more immediately available, we have provided numerous examples to illustrate our approach to practice in concrete descriptive detail. Therefore, following the description of each technical element of the overall approach, we have included one or more examples of dialogue drawn from our clinical cases. These have been taken verbatim from recordings of sessions; where that was not feasible, we have taken the liberty of paraphrasing or condensing pertinent transactions that have occurred in treatment. In addition, Chapters Nine, Ten, and Eleven consist of extensive excerpts from three cases, together with some explanatory comments.

We have also aimed for clarity at the level of style, in several ways. This work contains little of the technical jargon of psychiatry or psychology, most of which is foreign to our conceptual scheme. We have chosen to avoid the awkwardness inherent in such usages as "he/she"; instead, we explicitly note here that both therapists and clients may, of course, be male or female, and we sometimes use one pronoun and sometimes the other. For similar reasons, though our sessions may involve one or several persons, we have avoided the awkward form "client(s)" and simply use "client" to refer to the general case and "clients" when reference is specifically to a plural situation. Also, we have tried to avoid making verbal distinctions that we believe are unrealistic or invidious. For this reason, we may refer, interchangeably, to "the patient," "the client," "the complainant," or even to "the customer," and while from habit we usually write "the therapist," this could just as well be "the counselor."

Between Chapter One, on theory, and Chapters Nine, Ten, and Eleven, on case examples, our description of the technique itself is structured to match the chronological course of treatment. Since our treatment approach is strategic, Chapter Two is devoted to the general issue of therapist control over treatment—"Therapist Maneuverability." Then, in "Setting the Stage for Treatment," we deal with particular strategic considerations that may arise before treatment formally begins, most often in the telephone call the client makes to arrange for an appointment. The two chapters are placed early in the book because treatment is likely to go awry if the therapist is not in control of it, and issues of effective control can arise either in the initial phone contact or in the first minutes of the initial session.

After these "groundwork" chapters, we describe, in Chapter Four, the course most often taken in the first session—the initial interview. Most of this chapter deals with the specific information the therapist needs to resolve problems briefly and with how to elicit that information. Information special to our approach is taken up in Chapter Five, which elaborates on client sensibility (or client frame of reference)—"Patient Position." This focus is intimately related to the general issue of therapist influence and is the basis for enhancing compliance with interventions and avoiding patient resistance.

However, if one is to intervene purposefully and effectively, one has to review strategic information, devise a goal of treatment, and formulate a strategy to achieve that goal. Accordingly, Chapter Six, "Case Planning," deals with procedures for doing so. Once the therapist has formulated a goal of treatment and has devised a basic strategy, he will need guidelines for implementing that strategy—tactics. For that purpose, Chapter Seven, "Interventions," describes general and specific suggestions, assignments, and postures the therapist can use in resolving the client's problem, as well as in maintaining a tactical advantage in treatment. The descriptive part of our work then concludes with Chapter Eight, on the termination of treatment.

Chapters Nine, Ten, and Eleven illustrate the overall approach as it has been used in our own clinical cases, by offering extensive excerpts of dialogue from each of three cases, so that the reader can see how the "package" is put together. Interspersed with the segments of dialogue is our own commentary explaining the rationale of the particular moves the therapist has made—a sort of "thinking out loud" for the purpose of making the course of the ongoing treatment clearer.

An inherent outgrowth of our view of problems is the blurring of the usual distinction between clinical problems and problems encountered in many other spheres of human activity. Therefore, even though this book is devoted to psychotherapy, we have included a final chapter (Chapter Twelve) on the relevance of our approach to those problems lying beyond the conventional bounds of psychotherapy. We believe that the inclusion of such a chapter will further clarify our basic framework as well as stimulate those readers whose work may, at times, bring them into contact with nonclinical problems.

As the reader will note, our work reflects an orientation more like that of a chess game than that implied by the traditional emphasis on "therapeutic relationship." We know that the psychotherapy literature traditionally focuses more on the "needs" of the patient and less on the specific tactics of the therapist. Certainly, the matter of therapist control of treatment has been almost totally avoided in discussions of psychotherapy. We realize that there is a risk of appearing callous when one makes explicit a strategy-oriented approach—when one exposes "the tricks of the trade," so to speak. But this obviously is a risk we have felt it important to take. In our own ethical framework, if a strategic or manipulative approach can shorten the patient's suffering and can save him time and money, it is not an immoral stance. Moreover, we believe that avoiding investigation and explicit discussion of how therapists actually deal with their patients has helped maintain an unfortunate aura of obscure complexity and magic, in which the resolution of patients' problems necessarily is seen as an art. Instead, we feel that treatment is, or at least should be, much more a craft, albeit one to which the individual therapist can lend any artistry she possesses. With artistry alone, one can only stand in awe of the "gifted" therapist; with therapy viewed as a craft, one can learn to replicate effective problem-solving techniques.

In a number of sections throughout the book, we have

made reference to other therapeutic approaches. These references are not to be taken as adequate characterizations of those therapies but are given as comparisons for the purpose of making *our* views as clear as possible. Finally, we do not see our work as the last word: Since there is always change in human living, this will never be written. Our interest in this book, as it has been in our training sessions, is not to promote our approach as final but to make it clear enough so that it can form a basis on which each therapist can build and develop further improvements and refinements.

Any work of this kind reflects contributions by numerous people other than the authors, and to them we are deeply indebted. In addition to earlier contributors mentioned in *Change* and in our first article on this work (Weakland and others, 1974), we must mention particularly those current members of the Brief Therapy Center whose work has provided valuable help in clarifying what we have been and are about: Paul Watzlawick, Eldon Evans, Neil Brast, James Coyne, and Vincent Moley, and others who have, in recent time, worked along with us in providing their own useful perspectives: Allen VanderWell, Varda Salomon, and Renée Sabourin.

We are also grateful to attendees of our workshops and readers of *Change,* who stimulated the writing of this work by their questions about technique and requests for more explicit guidance in translating the general principles of *Change* into specific guidelines for treatment.

Finally, Sharon Lucas has been invaluable in efficiently making transcripts from taped case material and transforming none-too-legible sections of manuscript into clear typescript.

Palo Alto, California   Richard Fisch
April 1982   John H. Weakland
                                                           Lynn Segal

❧ Contents ❧

❧ The Authors ☙

Richard Fisch, M.D., is in the private practice of psychiatry in Palo Alto, California, is director and principal investigator of the Brief Therapy Center of the Mental Research Institute, and is a research associate of that institute. He holds a part-time position as psychiatric consultant to the Juvenile Probation Department of San Mateo County and is a clinical assistant professor of psychiatry at Stanford University School of Medicine.

Fisch received his B.A. degree in 1949 from Colby College and his M.D. degree in 1954 from the New York Medical College. After an internship completed in 1955 at the Beth El (now Brookdale) Hospital in Brooklyn, New York, he took his psychiatric residency from 1955 to 1958 at the Sheppard and Enoch Pratt Hospital in Towson, Maryland. He received his certification from the American Board of Psychiatry and Neurology in 1962.

From 1957 to 1958, he was assistant chief of service at

the Sheppard and Enoch Pratt Hospital and, from 1958 to 1959, served as associate director of the psychiatric inpatient service at San Mateo County Hospital. He entered private practice in 1959. His association with the Mental Research Institute began in 1962, when he served as a member of the Family Training Committee. Through the years he has pursued his interest in family therapy and, beginning in 1965, in researching methods of shortening treatment. In 1981 he received an award from the American Family Therapy Association for distinctive achievement in new directions in family therapy. Among his publications relevant to the area covered in this book are "Resistance to Change in the Psychiatric Community" (*Archives of General Psychiatry,* October 1965); "On Unbecoming Family Therapists," with P. Watzlawick, J. Weakland, and A. Bodin, in A. Ferber and others (Eds.), *The Book of Family Therapy* (New York: Science House, 1972); "Brief Psychotherapy: Focused Problem Resolution," with J. Weakland, P. Watzlawick, and A. Bodin (*Family Process,* June 1974); *Change: Principles of Problem Formation and Problem Resolution,* with P. Watzlawick and J. Weakland (New York: Norton, 1974); "Hyperactivity Resolved by Brief Psychotherapy," with J. Weakland, in D. M. Ross and S. A. Ross (Eds.), *Hyperactivity: Theory, Research and Action* (New York: Wiley, 1976); "Sometimes It's Better for the Right Hand Not to Know What the Left Hand is Doing," in P. Papp (Ed.), *Family Therapy: Full Length Case Studies* (New York: Gardner Press, 1977); "The Impact of Milton Erickson on Brief Psychotherapy," in J. K. Zeig (Ed.), *Ericksonian Approaches to Hypnosis and Psychotherapy* (New York: Brunner/Mazel, in press).

John H. Weakland, a licensed marriage, family, and child counselor, is in private practice in Palo Alto, California. He is also a research associate of the Mental Research Institute, associate director of the Brief Therapy Center of the institute, and clinical assistant professor in the Department of Psychiatry and Behavioral Sciences, Stanford University School of Medicine.

Weakland was originally trained as a chemist and chemical engineer at Cornell University, receiving his degrees in 1939 and 1940, respectively. After six years of engineering practice in research and plant design, he returned to graduate school for work in anthropology and sociology at the New School for Social Research and Columbia University, from 1947 to 1952; his research centered primarily on culture and personality and on the Chinese family and culture, and he worked under Gregory Bateson, Margaret Mead, and Ruth Benedict.

In 1953, he moved to Palo Alto to work on Gregory Bateson's research projects on human communication, together with Jay Haley, Don D. Jackson, and William F. Fry, Jr. This research led to the "double-bind" theory of schizophrenia, the West Coast beginnings of family therapy, and the founding of the Mental Research Institute by Jackson.

Weakland is a fellow of the American Anthropological Association and of the Society for Applied Anthropology and is an advisory editor of *Family Process*. In 1981 he received an award for distinctive achievement in new directions in family therapy from the American Family Therapy Association. He is the author or coauthor of fifty professional papers and four books: *Change: Principles of Problem Formation and Problem Resolution,* with P. Watzlawick and R. Fisch (New York: Norton, 1974); *The Interactional View: Studies at the Mental Research Institute, Palo Alto, 1956-1974,* ed. with P. Watzlawick (New York: Norton, 1977); *Counseling Elders and Their Families,* with J. J. Herr (New York: Springer, 1979); and *Rigor and Imagination: Essays from the Legacy of Gregory Bateson,* ed. with Carol Wilder-Mott (New York: Praeger, 1981).

Lynn Segal, a licensed clinical social worker, is a research associate of the Mental Research Institute (MRI) and a member of that institute's Brief Therapy Project. He received his B.A. degree in psychology from Hofstra University (1966) and his M.S.W. degree in social work from Adelphi University (1968). He was the recipient of the Don D. Jackson Memorial Award in 1977, was one of the organizers and co-leaders of the El Camino Hospital Pain Program, and is past chairman of the MRI Training Committee. Presently, he divides his professional time between training others in brief therapy and family systems work, doing research in psychotherapy, and maintaining a private practice in Palo Alto. He has conducted training workshops throughout the United States and in Europe.

Segal's most recent publications include: "Focused Problem Resolution," in E. Tolson and W. J. Reid (Eds.), *Models of Family Treatment* (New York: Columbia University Press, 1981); "The 'D' Family: A Failure to Assess Customership," with P. Watzlawick, in S. B. Coleman (Ed.), *Failures in Family Therapy* (New York: Guilford Publications, in press).

Segal's professional interests are currently focused on reexamining the application of general systems theory to clinical practice: the use of video tape examples, taken from film, plays, and television, to facilitate the teaching of brief therapy and the interactional view; and exploring the possibilities of integrating brief therapy with more "traditional" models of treatment.

The Tactics
of Change

*Doing Therapy
Briefly*

❧ 1 ❧

Practice — and Theory

This is a practical book about the deliberate promotion of useful change, particularly in psychotherapy. That is, its specific focus is on *what* to do and *how* to do it in order to help resolve persistent human problems effectively and efficiently.

Yet the matter is not quite that simple and limited. Details of procedure do not stand by themselves. They are related to some rationale of treatment, which must be known if procedures are to be understood and evaluated. This is especially important with our treatment approach, since the "whats" and "hows" we will be proposing here often are out of the ordinary. Consider this brief example, summarized from the concluding section of our second interview with a thirty-year-old professional woman:

Patient: My main problem is that I'm depressed most of the time. It has its ups and downs—at the worst, I'm still just able to do my job, but nothing else; at the best, I still don't feel good.

1

Therapist: You say depression is your main problem. Anything else?

Patient: Yes—I don't have any lasting relationships with men. They're all brief and unsatisfying.

Therapist: Could you describe that a bit more specifically?

Patient: Well, when I'm feeling relatively OK, I'll take some action to find somebody. I may go to a bar and meet a man there.

Therapist: Then what?

Patient: After we get acquainted, we may go home together. But it never lasts long. After a few days or a week—a couple of weeks at most—I don't hear from him anymore. And if I call him, he puts me off. Then I wonder what's the matter with me, and I get depressed again. This happens over and over.

Therapist: Are you depressed right now?

Patient: Yes—and I'd like to feel better.

Therapist: I can understand that. But I have to tell you that it really would not be a good thing for you to start feeling better, less depressed, right away. Let me explain why, since I know this may seem contradictory to you because you came here to get over your depression. You see, you have another problem: In some way—it's not yet clear just how—at this point, you don't know how to handle your relationships with men so that they work out to your satisfaction. In that particular area, you must lack some social skill you need. So, if your depression were to get better right away—before you have time to find out what you need to handle things better—then you would be in serious danger of getting involved with another man, only to have it end badly soon. And then you'd feel even more depressed.

Patient: Well, I can sort of see that, even though I'd like to feel better.

Therapist: Of course you would, but right now it's too big a danger for you. In fact, I'm concerned that if you got to feeling even a little better, you might be tempted to go out looking, and fall into a bad relationship despite what I've explained to you. So let me suggest a way to prevent that. If you should feel an urge or need to go out, OK, you may have to. But you definitely should do something to make yourself less attractive, so as to prevent or at least slow down this quick involvement in relationships—until we can get an idea of what you need to have them work out better. You don't have to do very much. If you do go out, you could just make a black mark somewhere on your face—as a sort of blemish.

Given only this information, most people, including professional counselors, would probably regard the therapist's concluding remarks as strange—perhaps stranger than the behavior of many patients. Telling a depressed woman not to feel better and to deliberately mar her appearance does not make common sense. Neither does it fit with commonly held ideas about psychopathology and therapy—for instance, that patients need support and encouragement. Therefore, this therapist's behavior is likely to be considered simply illogical and quixotic, and to be dismissed out of hand—if not censured.

One might, however, pursue the case further and observe the patient's response to the therapist's statement, reported in the next session two weeks later:

Therapist: Maybe you'd just kind of fill me in on where you are at this point.

Patient: OK. Well [in a bright voice], I don't know whether I was at the end of my depression or what, but the suggestion given two weeks ago that I be very cautious about relationships because I really didn't know what I was doing, and so to—if necessary—even do something to enforce the fact that I shouldn't go into them too quickly. Well, I didn't see myself as needing a special kind of blemish, or whatever you could call it, to keep me out of relationships, because I don't see myself as really having to do that in order to keep people away. I see myself as doing a good job without intentionally setting anything up. Maybe that wasn't the purpose of it, but that's the way I interpreted it. Anyway, just that thought—that I really didn't know what I was doing, and maybe I should be cautious—uh—made me feel really good—and I kind of went around thinking, "I don't have to [laughs], you know, meet someone; I don't have to have this wonderful relationship; I can just take care of myself," and—uh—it's like doctor's orders that I should stay away from this—this thing. And so I've been feeling pretty good for the past couple of weeks. And that was kind of a surprise to me; I didn't know that it would have that effect. But as I say, I don't know; could be that I was at the tail end of what—maybe I was at the tail end of the depression. But I know when I thought about that, you know, "Beware of —" it somehow lightened me, rather than making me feel deprived.

Therapist: It lightened you to think, OK, maybe you should go slow about . . .

Patient: Yeah.

Therapist: . . . getting into new relationships . . .

Patient: Yeah.

Therapist: . . . or rekindling old ones?

Patient: Yeah—I wonder—at the time, though—and even now—I'm not quite sure what "Go slow" meant—uh—but that didn't seem to matter—in terms of the reaction I had to the—uh—the thing.

Therapist: Um.

Patient: So . . .

Therapist: Well—uh—a couple of questions. One, you say you're not sure whether the thing was ending already or what, but you felt lighter since—that session—I think were the words you used.

Patient: Um-hm.

Therapist: Are you implying, then, that you feel you're not depressed anymore?

Patient: Uh—

Therapist: Or that you're feeling better?

Patient: Well, I don't feel depressed like I was then. That was kind of—uh—hard to work, to eat, to move myself from place to place—and I haven't felt like that. I just kind of go along the way I have been—which is not, you know, manic, or—maybe people would look at me and think I was depressed, but I feel I am at my normal state.

From this verbatim statement, it appears that what the therapist said in the previous interview had a positive effect, despite its strangeness. His approach therefore might be worth emulating, even if it is not comprehensible. While this conclusion might represent some advance over the previous uncomprehending rejection, since it takes more data into account, it could lead at most to blind copying—or, more realistically, to attempted copying in a field where no two cases or situations are ever precisely the same. Only by understanding the general conceptions of problems and treatment—in short, the theory—to which specific practices are related can one go beyond such blind response, either to judiciously reject or judiciously accept and apply such an approach to therapy.

The importance of this relationship between theory and practice can hardly be overemphasized. All purposive human behavior depends greatly on the views or premises people hold, which govern their interpretation of situations, events, and relationships. For the particular domain of behavior called psychotherapy, this means that the ideas or premises a person holds concerning the nature of problems and treatment will strongly influence the kind of data he will focus attention on, whom he will see in treatment, what he will say and do—and, equally, *not* say or do—with the patient and others involved, and, not least, how he will evaluate the results of such actions.

For example, in other times and places, bizarre behavior has often been interpreted as the result of demonic possession; accordingly, it was treated by some rite of exorcism. In our society today, similar behavior is more apt to be taken as indicating the presence of a mental disease—schizophrenia, for example—and it is therefore concluded that some medical or psychological therapy should be applied. But just what this therapy should consist of—hospitalization, brain surgery, drugs, individual psychotherapy, family therapy—will vary further according to whether the "disease" is conceived to be physiological, biochemical, psychological, or interactional in origin and nature. Obviously, such differences in conceptions of the problem also make for considerable differences in prognosis—not only what sort of therapy is at issue but how drastic and lengthy it is expected necessarily to be. Finally, evaluation of the results of treatment also will depend on one's conception of the problem. For example, schizophrenia may be conceived of as an inherent and fundamental defect in an individual, so that even if the peculiar behavior ceases, the patient will, at best, be forever labeled "a schizophrenic in remission"—whereas, from another point of view, he would now be considered no longer schizophrenic. Schizophrenia, of course, is an extreme example; but for all other problems, even the apparently mildest or simplest, the significance of the views held by the therapist is similar.

Obviously, then, we see theory as important and indeed necessary for the practice of therapy. Yet—in either of two ways—theory can also lead to difficulties and errors (Weakland, 1978; Whitaker, 1976; Haley, 1978). First, theory may be over-elaborated or taken too seriously—reified—until it hampers direct observation and simple interpretation of behavior. To avoid this, our presentation of theory will be as brief and simple as possible, and deliberately limited in scope and concept. (For more on our theoretical views and their significance for practice, see Weakland and others, 1974; Watzlawick, Weakland, and Fisch, 1974; Herr and Weakland, 1979.) We do not see theory as necessarily something elaborate, complex, or final—not a higher truth or ultimate reality, somehow beyond what is directly observable—but, rather, as only a set of relatively general ideas or views which are useful in integrating particulars of observation and action in a systematic and comprehensible way. Moreover, although one could always speculate about possible broader implications of our approach, like any other, we are not attempting here to present a comprehensive theory of human nature, of human existence, or "the mind" but only to state our general conception of the nature of problems that people bring to therapists, and a corresponding conception of effective intervention to resolve such problems—a theory as close as possible to practice.

In short, our theory is just a conceptual map of our approach to understanding and treating the kinds of problems therapists meet in daily practice. Like any map, it is basically a tool to help someone find his way from one place to another—in this case from the therapist's encountering a client's problem to its successful resolution. As a tool, a map is never the actuality, is always provisional, and is to be judged primarily by the results of its use. Yet a good map can be very useful in clarifying the lay of the land and in orienting one's course amid the fog, swamps, and thickets so prevalent in the land of human problems.

We also aim to make our fundamental views—our premises and assumptions—as explicit as possible, since the other danger from theory arises when it is inexplicit. Just as one cannot *not* communicate, since in a social setting even silence is a message, one cannot *not* theorize. We all have general ideas which form the context for, and thus guide, our specific thinking and behavior. But these general views may be implicit and taken for granted. Then they are all the more influential, since they are less open to review, questioning, and possible revision. If one loses his way in therapy while following an implicit map —if indeed he can even recognize that he has lost his way—he can only try one tack after another, rather randomly, or label the patient as "untreatable." Therefore, we will attempt to make our premises and assumptions, and their relationship to our practices, as clear and explicit as we can. This is all the more important since many of our premises, like our practices, will be unfamiliar and unusual.

While we believe that our premises, taken together, constitute a unified and consistent view of the nature of problems and their resolution, this view did not spring into being full grown and complete, nor is it unique to us except in certain significant respects—particularly its cohesive structure and its emphasis on the role of attempted solutions to problems. Rather, it is the outcome of the extensive modification of earlier views by experience, reflection and change over a long period. A brief summary of this developmental background, outlining prior views that we have abandoned or modified, may help in making our present view more clear and accessible by contrast.

We began from an immersion, by training and experience, in psychodynamic concepts and related practices. Psychodynamic theory focuses on the individual patient, especially on intrapsychic structures and processes. Consequently, its emphasis is not primarily on whatever behavior a problem involves but on presumed underlying matters. Moreover, this viewpoint sees the present mainly as the resultant of the past, in terms of linear chains of cause and effect, from origins to consequences. This adds up to an emphasis on what is beneath and behind, long ago and far away, instead of here and now. This emphasis on hidden origins instead of what is presently observable necessarily leads to extensive inquiry about the past and to heavy use of inference. In addition, this view tends strongly, though often implicitly, toward viewing problems as the result of deficits in the individual's makeup—deficits resulting (except for the innate deficiencies sometimes posited) either from the lack of early positive experiences or from negative experiences, early or late. With regard to practice, it follows that the therapist first must achieve an understanding of such complex and hidden matters and then must help the patient, by interpretations, to achieve adequate understanding. Support and guidance aimed at overcoming or compensating for a presumed deficit may also be important in some forms of individual treatment, but the fundamental curative factor still is supposed to be "insight"; the basic premise is the intellectual one "Knowledge will make one free."

All of us, however, then became involved in the family therapy movement. And family therapy is not just a matter of different specific practices—seeing whole families instead of separate individuals. Instead, its view of problems and their professional treatment differs from the psychodynamic position just outlined, point by point. Obviously, family therapy focuses on the identified patient not alone but in his primary social context, the family. A focus on communication and interaction within the family leads to much more emphasis on actual behaviors, what is observably going on in the present, rather than on the past, the internal, and the inferential. Viewing problem behavior not in isolation but in relation to its immediate context —the behavior of other family members—means more than just a specific change of viewpoint, important as that is. This change exemplifies a general shift in epistemology from a search for linear cause-and-effect chains to a cybernetic or systems viewpoint—the understanding and explanation of any selected bit of behavior in terms of its place in a wider, ongoing, organized system of behavior, involving feedback and reciprocal reinforcement throughout. Also, this shift toward focusing on how a system may be organized or functioning poorly implies less belief in individual deficits. For practice, this view proposes that the therapist's task is not just to understand the family system and the place of the problem within it but also to take action to change the malfunctioning system in order to resolve the problem.

Growing experience with what might now be called "conventional family therapy," however, led us to realize that not much explicit attention was being paid to the various means that therapists might use to promote change. Though different therapists had different styles, and some specific techniques were described in isolation, there was little discussion of the general problem of how to change behavior, deliberately, in human systems. The situation was much the same concerning just what behavior should be the target of change efforts. There was the basic notion that changes elsewhere in a family system would be required if the problem behavior was to be altered, but guidelines on where the therapist should focus inquiry and influence toward change were fragmentary and conflicting. This notion led to the view that rather sweeping revision of family organization and functioning is needed to resolve problems—a view accompanied by the practice of routinely seeing nothing less than the whole family, and consequently the elaboration and lengthening of family treatment.

The Brief Therapy Center began its work fifteen years ago with a few simple ideas running counter to the trends just listed. Our goal was to see what could be done in a strictly limited period—a maximum of ten one-hour sessions—by focusing on the main presenting complaint, maximally utilizing any active techniques for promoting change that we knew or could borrow from others (such as Milton Erickson, Don Jackson, and

Jay Haley), and searching for the minimum change required to resolve the presenting problem rather than aiming to restructure whole families. From the beginning, we worked as a team. One member was assigned as therapist for each case, and the other members observed all sessions through a one-way mirror. The observers could offer comments or suggestions over an intercom phone, or even by entering the treatment room temporarily. All sessions were audiotaped to make detailed study possible. The experience gained in working this way, together with extensive discussion and efforts to generalize and make explicit what we were doing in practice, eventually resulted in our present premises. We see these views as representing a further pursuit and development of some of the most basic ideas in family therapy, though others might see them as a departure from it.

It is our task to make these views and their relationships plain, but we need and ask our readers' cooperation in this, mainly by suspending judgment temporarily. We can describe our ideas and practices only gradually, piece by piece. It is a natural temptation similarly to examine what we say piecemeal, especially by comparison with or translation into terms of some other existing view of problems and therapy. But this will only make it harder to perceive, and *then* to evaluate, our approach as such. Much of our own effort in formulating our views has been a matter of achieving detachment from such existing conceptions. Perhaps it might help the reader to look on what we are about to describe, at least at first, as a fanciful map of a new *terra incognita,* rather than an account of any known land. Here, then, is our map.

Our most basic view—indeed, a metaview, to which all the rest are subsidiary—is already suggested in what was said earlier about theory and maps generally. Nevertheless, because this view is different both from what is commonly held implicitly and what is stated explicitly by scholars in fields ranging from theology to the sciences (though it is increasingly being questioned in science nowadays), it bears very specific repetition: We are talking *only* of views, not of reality or of truth, because we believe that views are all we have, or ever will have. It is not even a question of views that are more or less real or true, or progressively approaching the truth. Some views may be more useful or effective than others in accomplishing one's chosen end, but this is a pragmatic criterion, not one of "reality." The analogy of languages may help make this fundamental point clearer. There are many languages; all bear some orderly relationship to observation and experience, yet simultaneously are largely arbitrary conventional systems. One may be better for one purpose—English for modern scientific discourse—and another for a different purpose—Eskimo for distinguishing varieties of snow. But this does not make the one more real or true than the other.

Our view of what constitutes problems and useful help can be presented from the proverbial "Man from Mars" standpoint. That is, what would an intelligent but naive observer perceive as common and characteristic if he could look in on an adequate sample—especially initial interviews—of actual psychotherapy sessions? Though this may seem a superficial approach, it has the advantages of simplicity, concreteness, and minimization of presuppositions and inferences. We propose that such an observer would, over and over, note this:

1. A client expresses concern about some behavior—actions, thoughts, or feelings—of himself or of another person with whom he is significantly involved.
2. This behavior is described as (a) deviant—unusual or inappropriate to the point of abnormality—and (b) distressing or harmful, immediately or potentially, either to the behaver (the patient) or to others.
3. It is reported that efforts have been made by the patient or others to stop or alter this behavior, but they have been unsuccessful.
4. Therefore, either the patient or others concerned are seeking the therapist's help in changing the situation, which they have not been able to change on their own.

Our view of the nature of therapy and our general approach to practice follow directly from this conception of problems.

First, since we see problems as consisting of undesired behavior in the present, we attach little importance to presumed
underlying factors in the past or in the depths of the patient's
mind. We do attach importance to identifying clearly the problem behavior—what it is, in what way it is seen as a problem,
and by whom. We also attach importance to the performance
and persistence of the problem behavior. Behavior does not
exist independently on its own; it consists of acts performed by
some person. We recognize that a person may do or say something and disclaim that he is doing so, and such distinctions between "voluntary" and "involuntary" behavior may need recognition by therapists because they are important to clients. But
we do not ourselves see this separation as useful. Rather, we
consider all behavior, even the most bizarre acts or utterances
of schizophrenic patients, in the same light.

Moreover, to constitute a problem, a behavior must be
performed repeatedly. A single event may have unfortunate or
even disastrous consequences, but the event cannot itself be a
problem, since a problem by our definition is an ongoing difficulty. Worrying about possible recurrence of an unfortunate
event, in contrast, could constitute a problem—all the more if
such recurrence is unlikely.

Accordingly, the occurrence (especially the recurrence)
of specific behaviors is a major issue needing explanation. Our
view is that all behavior, normal or problematical—and whatever
its relations to the past or to individual personality factors—is
continually being shaped and maintained (or changed) primarily
by ongoing reinforcements in the particular behaving individual's system of social interaction. This especially includes the
family, though other systems of interaction, such as school and
work organizations, may also be important. That is, one person's
behavior instigates and structures another person's behavior, and
vice versa. If the two are in contact over time, repetitive patterns
of interaction will arise. For this reason, we attach great importance to the context of other behaviors in which the behavior
identified as constituting the problem occurs. What are those
behaviors, by the patient or others concerned, that may provoke, and by repetition maintain, the problem behavior? Mean-

while, of course, the problem behavior is likely to be provoking these related behaviors—interaction is basically circular, not a one-way street: The husband withdraws "because my wife nags," while the wife nags "because my husband withdraws," and a pattern of characteristic behaviors is maintained. We con-consider the interactive context of behavior so important that, in addition to giving little weight to historical or personality factors as presumed sources of problem behavior, we give little weight to presumed organic deficits unless these are definitely established and clearly relevant. Even then, we will attach considerable importance to how they are being dealt with behaviorally.

Next, there is the central question of the persistence of problems—not just ordinary behavior but undesired behavior—in the face of dissatisfaction and attempts at change. The views already stated suggest that problem-provoking behaviors must exist within the patient's system of social interaction and be repeatedly performed for a problem to exist and continue. But what are these problem-maintaining behaviors, how do they occur, and why are they persisted in, apparently paradoxically?

To become more specific, at this point we must add our clinical experience to our general views of behavior and interaction. This experience has indicated over and over—ironic as it may seem—that something in people's attempted "solutions," the very ways they are trying to alter a problem, contributes most to the problem's maintenance or exacerbation. We may summarize our view of both the origin and the persistence of problems in this way: Problems begin from some ordinary life difficulty, of which there is never any shortage. This difficulty may stem from an unusual or fortuitous event. More often, though, the beginning is likely to be a common difficulty associated with one of the transitions regularly experienced in the course of life—marriage, the birth of a child, going to school, and so on (see Weakland and others, 1974; Haley, 1973). Most people handle most such difficulties reasonably adequately—perfect handling is neither usual nor necessary—and thus we do not see them in our offices. But for a difficulty to turn into a problem, only two conditions need be fulfilled: (1) the difficulty is mishandled, and (2) when the difficulty is not resolved,

more of the same "solution" is applied. Then the original difficulty will be escalated, by a vicious-circle process (see Maruyama, 1963; Wender, 1968), into a problem—whose eventual
size and nature may have little apparent similarity to the original difficulty.

The following case excerpt, for example, illustrates how a
serious concern about sexual performance—previously reasonably satisfying—arose out of a conversation between a young
woman and her female friends and was then maintained and
exacerbated by becoming a focus of interactive concern between this woman and her husband:

Patient: Before I was married, I don't think I . . . Or I didn't
realize I'd never had an orgasm, and I never thought about it.
You know, I'd tried sex, and that was fine, and just before I got
married I was informed by some friends of mine that I had
never had one. Well, we got to talking about it, and I realized
I'd never had one. And . . .

Therapist: I was going to say, they told you . . .

Patient: In our discussions it came out. I realized that I'd never
had one. And then it became a problem. And sex was just no
longer really enjoyable. 'Cause I kept, you know, waiting for
this other to happen, or at one point it was so scientific that,
you know, it was like there was no pleasure. It was just step by
step—to the point where for several months we didn't have any
relationship at all.

Therapist: If we could kind of go in sequence, you know—you
found out you didn't have orgasms. What have you tried?

Patient: Then we tried really examining my body and figuring
out where everything was. And this was the first stage, and what
to manipulate, and discovering the clitoris. And that didn't
work. We were both—well, especially I was proccupied with having an orgasm and what we were doing, step by step by step.
Then it just became a pain. I mean, there was no spontaneity.
There was no joy in it at all. It was just a process that we went
through. The next thing we did was that we talked to friends.
We had another couple that we were very close to. And we
talked about the possibilities of things that we were doing

wrong, and whatever. And they were helpful, really, in telling us about different positions, things that might be easier. My husband's quite a bit bigger than I—things that might make it easier for me to open—and that helped a little bit. I think things got a little bit better, not as bad as the other thing.

Therapist: What gave you the idea, in talking to them, that you were not having an orgasm?

Patient: Oh, firecrackers didn't go off, and there wasn't this big ... When they were talking about it, it was like, after this happened, then you would feel, I don't know, they would talk about this series of peaks, you know, that you would peak and come down, and your body would do something, and I just knew that never happened. I knew that there was one time, I remember, you know, really, I felt like I had really been very close to it, you know, when I stopped to think back on previous experiences. And that was interrupted. I guess just from what they were describing, I didn't fit. What I had experienced just didn't fit with what they were describing.

Therapist: OK, so what they were having wasn't what your experience was.

Patient: Yeah.

Such a simple view of problems may be comprehensible yet hard to accept. It is not difficult to imagine that people may deal with life difficulties inappropriately, but how can substantial numbers of people not only make such errors but persist in them despite their own experience that their solutions are not working? Some explanatory scheme is needed to deal with this difficulty. This is a major function of the concept of "mental illness"; individuals act "irrationally," behaving in strange and nonproductive ways because they have some mental defect or deficit. In addition, ideas about unconscious motivation, secondary gain from symptoms, and fixation of character at an early age serve the same explanatory function more specifically. In the family therapy field, emphases on homeostasis, interpersonal advantages gained from problem behaviors, and so on, serve the same purpose.

Our view is quite different. We do not believe that persistence in inappropriate handling of difficulties must require either fundamental defects in family organization or mental deficits in the individual actors. Rather, we believe that people persist in actions that maintain problems inadvertently, and often with the best of intentions. Indeed, people may get caught in such repetitive behavior even when they are aware that what they are doing is not working, as indicated in an example involving parental attempts to control a delinquent child's behavior:

Therapist: I'd like to check out one thing: You're saying that with Jennifer you'd set some limits about the time that she should be home.

Mother: Oh, definitely, yes.

Therapist: Could you give me some idea about how you usually go about that?

Mother: Well, we have—and for all of the kids, you know, unless it's something particular. I mean, if something special should arise—with Jenny, that she has to be home on the weekdays. As a matter of fact, I don't let the kids out of the house during the week unless it's a school activity, or, you know, say, one of their friends is having a birthday or something. You know, unless it's something special. On those occasions, when they do go out, they must be home at 10:00. On the weekends, their curfew is 12:00 unless, again, it's some, you know, specific thing that I know is going on and they can't possibly be home by 12:00. Now Jenny, basically, has been grounded for a very long time. A lot of good it's done, but she has been grounded.

Therapist: When you say grounded, what kind of disciplinary measures do you institute when she's grounded?

Mother: She, you know, absolutely cannot—well, this is what I say—she's not supposed to leave the house; her telephone privileges are taken away from her; I guess basically that's about it.

Therapist: And when she breaks those rules, what happens then? Like if she does make phone calls or she does go out when she's grounded. How do you handle that?

Mother: I just extend her grounding; I don't know what else to do with her now.

Therapist: Well, could you give me a for instance of when Jennifer has broken one of these rules? Would you both talk to her together, or how is that handled?

Father: Generally not. If she breaks a rule and I happen to be there—and about the only rule she breaks that I'm aware of, or that I involve myself in is if she—is the telephone rule. And I usually have a fit. And tell her not to do that. She insists on using the phone in our bedroom, which I've asked her not to use. In fact, I've told her specifically, "Do not use." There are two other phones in the house, and it's not necessary to use our phone. And, in fact, she did that as recent as last night. And I just, you know, come down on her: "Jenny, I've told you time and time again, do not use that phone. And I mean do not use the phone." That's the extent of it.

Therapist: And what does she say when you've said that?

Father: OK.

Therapist: She just says "OK"?

Father: Yes. Or I'll ask her, "Jenny why are you in there using the phone? I've told you a hundred times, do not use the phone." "Gee, I don't know. I forgot." And it usually drops there. And we get the standard "I don't know" answer from all of them and so we accept that.

Mother: You know, what do you do? You can only say no and ground them for so long. And she knows it. Well, she doesn't even care if we put her on groundment anymore 'cause she just takes off and does what she wants to anyway. So that means absolutely nothing to her at this point in time.

Father: The whole thing is ineffectual. And we're playing games with each other now, and that's ridiculous.

Such persistence, as we see it, is most often a matter of logical error, in a very literal sense. It is not so much that people are illogical but that they logically pursue courses derived from incorrect or inapplicable premises, even when the premises do not work in practice. They follow poor maps very carefully, and this is quite expectable for people who are understandably anxious in the midst of difficulties. Belief in such maps may also make it hard to see that they are not serving as effective guides; it is easy to rationalize away direct experience of continuing trouble: "It is only our present efforts that keep things from being even worse." Moreover, there is a good supply of poor maps—or maps that apply only in limited circumstances and not in other but apparently similar ones—ready to hand. Worse yet, many such maps themselves appear quite logical or are heavily supported by tradition and conventional wisdom. Perhaps the most common and general such traditional map bears directly on our point here: "If at first you don't succeed, try, try again." In our own view, if at first you don't succeed, you might perhaps try a second time—but if you don't succeed then, try something *different.*

A general example may illustrate several of these interrelated points. If a person is feeling low and depressed, it is both humane and logical to offer support and encouragement—that is, some form of "Cheer up, things are not as bad as they seem, tomorrow will be brighter." This may be effective; if so, fine. However, it also may not be, for many possible reasons. For instance, the depressed person may disqualify this, saying to himself, "They're only saying that to make me feel better" or, worse, "They don't understand how I really feel" and become more depressed as a result. That is, what works or fails to work —observable responses—should take precedence over what is abstractly right or logical.

Our view of treatment and problem resolution is a counterpart of this view of the nature and persistence of problems. If problem formation and maintenance are seen as parts of a vicious-circle process, in which well-intended "solution" behaviors maintain the problem, then alteration of these behaviors should interrupt the cycle and initiate resolution of the problem —that is, cessation of the problem behavior, since it is no longer being provoked by other behaviors in the system of interaction. (In some cases, the therapist might consider it more appropriate to aim at changing the negative evaluation placed on the problem behavior, which of course is another piece of behavior; he may judge that a client is "making a federal case" out of a minor matter.) Furthermore, there is always the possibility that an initially small change in the vicious-circle interaction, appropriately and strategically directed, may initiate a beneficent circle, in which less of the "solution" leads to less of the problem, leading to less of the "solution" and so on. Therefore, we consider that a therapist's primary aim need not be to resolve all difficulties but to initiate such a reversal. This also means that even severe, complex and chronic problems are potentially open to effective resolution by brief and limited treatment.

Given this conception of problems and their resolution, the therapist must be an active agent of change. Not only must he get a clear view of the problem behavior and of the behaviors that function to maintain it; he must also consider what the most strategic change in the "solutions" might be and take steps to instigate these changes—in the face of the clients' considerable commitments to continuing them. This is the job of the therapist as we see it; the rest of this book will discuss how it may be done.

✻ 2 ✻

Therapist
Maneuverability

If an ideal brief therapy patient existed, such a person would essentially say, "I will give you all the information you request, in a form you can understand clearly, seriously entertain any new ideas you have about my problem, try any proposed new behaviors outside the therapy hour, and work hard to bring into treatment any of my family or friends who might help solve my problem." Unfortunately, people who fit this description probably seldom end up being psychotherapy patients. Conversely, actual patients usually do not comply in one or more of these areas. In this sense, wittingly or unwittingly, they resist the therapist's attempts to conduct treatment. In our view, patients hinder therapeutic effort most often out of desperation or fear that the problem will get worse. Therefore, it is one thing to know how best to proceed in treatment; it is quite another to have the *freedom* to proceed in the way one thinks best—that is, to be able to implement one's best

21

judgment throughout the course of treatment. We call this freedom "therapist maneuverability" because freedom connotes a
relatively passive state that remains constant. Maneuverability
implies the ability to take purposeful action despite fluctuating
obstacles or restrictions. A therapist needs to keep his options
open as therapy progresses, shifting as needed during the course
of treatment.

It may seem cold and calculating to talk about ways of
controlling the process of treatment, but we believe it is evident, on a little reflection, that the client is not in a position to
know how his problem should best be approached—if he did,
why would he be seeking professional help? Accordingly, almost all therapies involve tactics for providing therapist control
of the course of treatment. However, the "managerial" aspects
of therapies are often passed over as simply part of the treatment process. In psychoanalysis, for example, the patient on
the couch does not have the option to observe his analyst, while
the analyst, sitting behind him, can observe the patient or not as
he chooses. These relative positions, however, are seen only as a
necessary part of the analytic process. Similarly, the concept of
"defenses" allows the analyst to disqualify the patient's disagreement with his interpretations; in fact, by labeling it "resistance," the analyst can use such disagreement to legitimize
the presumed accuracy of the interpretation. Thus, analytic theory gives the analyst the option of metacommunicating about
the patient's behavior while the analysand does not have that
same option, at least legitimately.

In pointing this out, we do not mean to disparage other
therapies, since we believe that procedures for managing treatment are necessary in *all* approaches. This is not for the arbitrary purpose of controlling, per se. Rather, it is ethically consistent with our view that the guidance of treatment is an
inherent responsibility of the therapist and that it is to the patient's detriment if the therapist abdicates this responsibility.
Effective and responsible use of such procedures, however, is
markedly reduced if they are left implicit in the "philosophy"
of the approach rather than stated plainly as deliberate and purposeful actions. For that reason, we hope in this chapter to

make clear our own tactics for maintaining therapist maneuverability and thus control over treatment. Because this is such a fundamental factor in treatment, especially in doing therapy briefly, we have placed this chapter early in our book.

How, then, does one go about maximizing therapist maneuverability? First, since the therapist's maneuverability depends on the comparative nonmaneuverability of the patient, the therapist—to put it bluntly—needs to maintain his own options while limiting those of the patient. The fundamental basis of such maneuverability lies in the therapist's recognition that the patient needs him more than he needs the patient. Whatever a therapist may do, whether intervening in a problem or managing the course of treatment, rests on the simple option of being able to terminate treatment. The therapist cannot deal effectively with patient resistance unless he is prepared to exercise this ultimate option should it become necessary. In being thus prepared, the therapist will find that he rarely needs to exercise this option. There are times in treatment when this basic understanding needs to be made explicit; for example, when the client attempts to impose restrictive conditions that would prevent any beneficial outcome:

Cl: I've come in just this once to tell you about my wife's condition. She will have nothing to do with any psychotherapist, and in her deluded mind she believes there's nothing wrong with her. So I don't want you to ask her to come in; it will only create a painful scene for me. No, the only way she can be involved in treatment is by my inviting you for dinner and passing you off as a friend from work. Then, while you are there, you can evaluate her mental condition and see how sick she is. Hopefully, you will be able to gain her trust; then after awhile, you will be able to treat her and straighten her out.

A therapist is unlikely to agree to such a blatantly collusive arrangement. If he did, he would have closed off almost all his options—when and where to see whom, under what framing or context, the frequency and scheduling of appointments, and so forth. Meanwhile, the husband could control the entire course of the treatment, since all those decisions would be his to make. Such an arrangement well nigh dooms treatment to failure; and, perhaps worse, the failure of such "treatment" could allow the husband to define his wife's condition as hopeless, since he could claim that he had made the proper effort.

If, on the other hand, the therapist does not want to allow treatment to begin under such an impossible handicap, virtually his only recourse in such a case is to threaten termination:

Th: While I appreciate your caution in pursuing help for your wife, wrongly or rightly I cannot bring myself to do something I firmly believe would be detrimental to you and her. The risks of boomeranging in trying such a subterfuge are too high, and the probable costs too great. I would be glad to see what I can do for your wife, but if you insist that I follow your plan, then I am not the person for you, and you might be better off with someone who is more willing to take risks with your own and your wife's welfare.

Should the husband agree to forgo his conditions for treatment, he will have acceded to the therapist's control over therapy, and the therapist will be able to proceed with enhanced maneuverability. However, should the husband refuse, the therapist, by terminating, would have avoided joining a doomed and perhaps destructive venture. Moreover, should the husband persist with another therapist and find that his approach does indeed fail as predicted, he is more likely to start any subsequent attempt at treatment on a less controlling basis.

Means of Enhancing Maneuverability

Timing and Pacing. In part, maneuverability depends on the therapist's using the option to pull back from a position he has taken with a patient or from a strategy he has begun to implement, rather than sticking to it at all costs. Usually he will want to exercise that option when he finds he is encountering significant resistance from the patient. If, instead, he persists in using a strategy that is not working, he is risking increased resistance to his suggestion or reduction of his credibility in the eyes of the patient. In practice, the therapist should not wait until there is obvious and strong resistance; instead, he should shift his tack as soon as he recognizes small but definite indicators that the strategy is not working. To avoid "getting in too deep," he can seek certain information first—to "test the waters," so to speak—before he begins any significant line of approach. Furthermore, he should check along the way to assess patient acceptance or nonacceptance of each step. That is, he will be *timing* and *pacing* his comments in accordance with the patient's responses. (This is similar to the step-by-step procedure in hypnosis: the hypnotist makes a small suggestion and then checks the subject's response before elaborating on that suggestion or giving an additional suggestion.)

When a client first comes in, the therapist usually knows little about his values, opinions, and priorities, all of which can have a bearing on dealing with the problem he is coming in about. One can seriously reduce one's maneuverability by taking a definite position prematurely, only to find it is aversive to the patient's sensibilities, values, or some deeply held viewpoint. The therapist's credibility and the client's compliance will be significantly reduced in such a situation. To rescue the treatment after such a blunder requires extra work and loss of time, especially if the error occurs early in treatment:

Th: I will need to ask some questions about your problem and what you hope to achieve in therapy. But I believe that therapy can be significantly shorter if we just stick to the present and focus on the behavioral elements of the problem. So first, what is happening currently that leads you to come in?

Pt: Well, I'd like to give you the information you want, but I've been having this trouble for many years and it has so disturbed the way I feel about myself that I assumed you would help me learn to understand why I feel the way I do. I've been feeling badly for so long I don't see how my problem can be handled in a short period of time. I'm really sorry; I didn't know you weren't interested in the kind of problem I have, and

I would appreciate it if you could direct me to a therapist who works with this kind of thing.

Th: [To parents and their teenage son] I know you are all here because you are each, in your own way, experiencing pain and that you would like to understand that and each other.

Son: Well, I'd like to say something.

Th: Yes, go ahead.

Son: The only pain I have is them [pointing thumb toward the parents]. They are always insisting I do stupid things: cut my hair, stay home all the time, do stupid homework—Jesus! They think I'm an infant, and now they want me to see a shrink! [Lapses into a sullen silence, glaring at his parents.]

Th: [To parents] Scott seems to be telling you how he hurts; that he has not gotten acknowledgment from you that he is an individual in his own right and his anger is a message that he badly needs recognition of his individuality. I'm wondering if that recognition is at all threatening to the two of you.

Father: Recognition of his individuality? Doctor, you have no idea what our home has become! There isn't a room that doesn't have his junk strewn all around. He comes and goes as he pleases. He doesn't do a lick of work to help out. My wife and I both work, and we are breaking our backs to make ends meet. We've given him most everything he wants, and then he either breaks or loses it and complains we never do anything for him! We haven't been able to have company over for almost a year now; the place is either a mess or he has his long-haired friends over playing their music so loud you can't think. Our home is not ours anymore, and if he doesn't get his way he raises hell. We have no authority in the home, and that's why we came here!

In the first example, the therapist is interested in doing brief, behaviorally oriented therapy, but he has made an error in timing: he has precipitously announced this orientation before learning that the patient has a very different view of what is required to resolve her problem. Thus, to her, the therapist appears to be impatient and indifferent to the seriousness of her problem and to her deep and painful feelings. She concludes that he is not capable of or interested in helping her. In the second example, the therapist immediately expresses his view that the parents and their son are there on a democratic and equal basis; in fact, by allowing the son to speak first and then legitimizing his complaint, he is actually putting the son on a superior footing. (We would not agree with either of these positions.) He then learns that the parents—certainly the father—have a very different view of treatment. They are there to gain some control over their son and their household, not to "understand" him nor give further ground.

In both examples, the therapist has either lost the case or seriously jeopardized further productive work by stating a firm position before checking out the patients' positions. To "hold one's fire" until one has checked on the patient's own views, and throughout treatment to take small steps and evaluate how each step is being received by the patient, is what we are referring to as "timing and pacing."

Ironically, in most other transactions in life, we automatically check things out before we plunge ahead. In therapy, strangely, there seems to be an implicit idea that normal practices of everyday intercourse are to be suspended and that therapists can operate without the usual social cautions they exercise in other aspects of their lives.

The procedures for gathering data in the initial session offer a ready opportunity to check out client sensibility without the therapist's having to take a premature stand, since he is "only asking questions" to become better informed and to understand the client. In that context, a number of questions, worded in the following manner, can be useful to elicit the client's position: (1) "You have been filling me in about the problem, and, at this point, I would appreciate your best guess as to *why* this problem exists?" (2) "I know some therapists say [such and such] about your problem. Have you had similar thoughts, or would that kind of thinking be all wet?" (3) "I'm not saying this would be appropriate for your problem, but I simply wonder if you have tried [such and such]?" Such questions enable the therapist to gain information about the client's views regarding his problem and the purpose of treatment, as well as to determine what range or approach the client is willing to entertain or, conversely, resist. At the same time, the questions do not commit the therapist, and they allow him to maintain his maneuverability, since he can easily back off from these probes if he encounters resistance from the client.

Taking One's Time. Maneuverability for the therapist also depends on his not being pressured to perform. In the face of client pressure, he needs to protect his option to take his time to think and plan. Patients may not intentionally put pressure on their therapist; yet often, in their distress and desperation, they generate a climate that urges the therapist to "do something, right now!" If the work of therapy is to proceed efficiently and constructively, the therapist should not be harried into making treatment decisions prematurely. In the long run, the time spent in avoiding such pitfalls will reduce the time spent in the overall treatment and is therefore consistent with the aim of doing treatment briefly.

There is no particular trick or expertise required in knowing *how* to take one's time. We are all familiar with and frequently use such rejoinders as "Well, let me think about that for awhile," "I'm afraid I don't have any answer to that right now," "I'm really not with it today. Maybe tomorrow I'll be sharper" to indicate to another that we are under no injunction to perform instantly. The difficult part of taking one's time is recognizing *when* one is under pressure, since a client's demands are likely to be implicit rather than explicit:

Cl: I know it must seem ridiculous but I can't get this damned thing off my mind. I keep going around on it so I can't think of anything else. [Client looks agitated.] I know I have to make a decision, one way or another, but I still keep going in circles. [Rubbing his palm on the arm of the chair and leaning forward] It's a damned dilemma. If I take the job, I will be letting my family down but if I don't [pauses] if I don't, I will be passing up just the opportunity I've been looking for. If I had all the time in the world, I could come up with the right decision but I just learned they want my answer by Wednesday—which is just two days off. [Looks expectantly at therapist.]

Here the client subtly pressures the therapist to help him make his decision right away, and perhaps to extend the session beyond the usual time. If the therapist attempts this task under such pressure, he is likely to become as rattled as his patient, which helps neither. To avoid this, the therapist should take his time:

Th: Yes, I can see your dilemma. [Commiseratingly] Hmmm. [Pause] No, I don't see a way out of it. [Pause] I'll tell you what. Let me think about it for a couple of minutes, since I just don't have any brilliant ideas right now. [Long pause] I'm sorry, Bob, but nothing comes to me. Since you said you have to come to some decision by Wednesday, the best I can offer is to meet with you tomorrow. But even then I might not be of help, and you may just have to flip a mental coin.

Even where pressure is more explicit, the context can make it difficult for the therapist to take his time:

Cl: [On the telephone] You know, when I left the session today, I really felt up in the air and I don't think anything got resolved. I realized that I forgot to mention something very important, and it's a thing that plays a key role. I can't wait another week to see you about this, and I know you would want to understand the situation I'm facing. You see, when I spoke to Larry about the vacation, he had just returned from seeing his mother and what I hadn't known—since he never tells me anything—is that the visit with her had gone . . .

Th: Mary, let me interrupt for a second. I appreciate your calling and wanting to fill me in, but, unfortunately, I'm one of those people who don't grasp things very well on the phone and I've never been able to do psychotherapy on the telephone either. Since you're saying it's important, then it deserves more than a phone conversation. I could meet with you before your next scheduled appointment. Then I think I could do it more justice.

In both cases, the therapist has opted for taking his time and is in a better position to plan more useful ways of aiding the patient to resolve the problem.

At times, when patients offer vague information at great length, a therapist will feel pressured and may be led into attempting interventions based on insufficient or misleading data. Similarly, a therapist may pursue certain areas of questioning, only to receive vague responses; he then may work harder and harder to get the patient to be clear while the patient works less and less. In such situations, taking one's time usually requires recognizing that one is working too hard and getting nowhere and that doing more of the same can only be counterproductive. At that point, the therapist can deal with the pressure to perform by adopting a position of apparent obtuseness: "I don't understand," "You lost me," "Sometimes it's best not to move hastily in a complex situation," and so forth. This nonstraining position puts the onus on the client to make himself clearer and to do the work he needs to. Taking this position also requires that the therapist resist the traditional view that one must always convey "empathy," "perceptivity," and "understanding." However, usually the therapist will communicate—verbally and nonverbally—that the lack of understanding is due to some presumed defect on his part. For example, he may apologize for being obtuse, but then ask the patient to repeat her statement.

Finally, there is a distinct disadvantage in believing that the therapist must stick to the time-honored treatment hour, no matter what. Sometimes an optimum stopping point might be reached in twenty or thirty minutes; if one feels pressure to fill out the remainder of the session, the impact of what has already been accomplished may be diluted.

In short, just as we encourage patients to take their time in resolving their problems, the therapist owes himself the judicious management of time in addressing himself to the tasks of treatment.

Use of Qualifying Language. Patients often ask questions that invite the therapist to take a committed position before he wishes to do so, or to take a position he does not wish to take at all: "Now, don't you agree that my husband is being unfair to me?" If the therapist says "Yes," he is validating the patient's viewpoint and entering into a coalition against her husband; but if he says "No," he is in for an argument or some disqualification by the patient. However, he can maintain a noncommittal maneuverability by responding in a qualified way: "Well, I have never met your husband; but judging from what you have told me, I think I would be inclined to agree with you." By making this kind of statement, the therapist maintains his maneuverability—his freedom to leave options open for himself—and, at the same time, appears to have taken a stand.

At many points in treatment, the therapist may wish to make some definite intervention or to give some assignment to the patient but is uncertain whether the strategy on which the intervention is based will work. Therefore, he does not want his credibility to depend on the success or failure of the intervention. If it does not work, he will want time to assess why it did not and to formulate a new strategy or a new tactic to implement the old strategy. For that reason, the suggestion can be put in qualified language: "I have a suggestion to make, but I'm not sure how much it will accomplish. It will depend on your ability to use your imagination and, perhaps, on your readiness to take a step toward improvement." The qualifications here are a bit more subtle than in the first example. The second part of the first sentence modifies the first part. The second sentence qualifies the appropriateness or legitimacy of the suggestion to follow, and the words used in both sentences—words such as *not sure, how much, ability, use imagination,* and *readiness to take a step*—are qualifications. The qualifications make it clear that the suggestion about to be given is appropriate but that its success will depend on the patient's efforts, rather than the appropriateness of the suggestion itself.

This kind of phrasing is in marked contrast to a less qualified statement: "I have a suggestion that will help you relax in social situations, and I know you are ready for that improvement." If the patient returns and says she followed the therapist's instructions for relaxing in social situations in just the way he described but was not one whit more relaxed, his credibility and thus his maneuverability are reduced, since he will have a harder time when he attempts to get her to accept another approach to her problem. If the therapist uses the qualified framing and the intervention does not go well, he can maintain that the patient was not able to use her imagination *well enough* or that she may not be ready to make a change in her problem. Conversely, if the patient returns reporting definite success with the suggestion, the therapist can then take the tack "Well, I was concerned that you might not be able to get anywhere with the suggestion, but I obviously underestimated your imagination and your ability to use it." By praising the patient, he is *implicitly* underscoring the appropriateness and effectiveness of his suggestion, and this can further commit the patient to it.

We are not saying that a therapist should never take a definite and qualified stand. Quite often it is important that he do so. What we are emphasizing is that the therapist should protect himself from taking an explicit stand before he has had ample time and information to judge *what* stand he wants to take and *when*. Qualified language is an important tool in implementing that option.

Getting the Client to Be Specific. Just as the therapist must be able to take a noncommitted or fluid position, the patient must be helped to take committed or nonfluid positions. That is, the maneuverability of the therapist is dependent on the nonmaneuverability of the client. If the client is not required to be clear and specific in his comments and his responses to the therapist, if he is not required to give other than hazy information, he can shift his own position as it may suit him; and his maneuverability will be increased to the detriment of the therapist's, and correspondingly to the detriment of his treatment. Vague information can pose a problem at any phase of treatment. For example, it often occurs when patients are asked to describe their goals of treatment. A parent might say, "Of course, our main concern is the trouble John has been having at school. So our goal would be that he have a better attitude toward his school work and really buckle down." A "better attitude" and "really buckle down" are vague. If the goals are left at this, there is a risk that the parent can discount some real improvement that his son has made: "Well, yes, his grades have gone from Fs to Cs, but I don't see that as any real improvement. He still complains about his teacher and homework, and

I'm sure that attitude holds him back from getting the grades he really could." This difficulty would have been less likely to develop if the therapist had pinned the clients down at the outset:

Th: When you say a better attitude and buckling down, I'm not sure what that would look like. Could you make it clearer?

Parent: Well, applying himself more; showing a greater interest in the work.

Th: How would you know his attitude changed? That's the part I have trouble seeing clearly.

Parent: Well, I think it would show up in his grades.

Th: Oh. OK. His grades are all *F*s now. What kind of grades would indicate to you that he had made a change in his attitude?

Parent: His getting passing grades, naturally.

Th: I believe in his school *D*s are a passing grade. Is that what you mean or all *A*s or just what?

Parent: Oh, no. He wouldn't have to get *A*s. We'd be very happy to see a grade *C* average or, at least, nothing lower than a *C* in any of his courses.

Th: All right. That's much clearer to me now.

This aspect of maneuverability—obtaining clear statements from the client—has its principal bearing in the initial session, when the therapist is obtaining most of the information he needs to plan treatment. However, it is by no means limited to that phase of treatment, since the therapist will always want clear and specific data from clients, whether the subject be a description of the problem, how they have been attempting to deal with it, what events have transpired between sessions, or how they have carried out any suggested assignments. In this last regard, it can make an enormous difference whether or not the therapist insists on a clear report. After the assignment of homework, patients may return to the next session claiming that they did what they were supposed to do but that it made

little or no difference in the problem. If they are asked to be
specific about *how* they carried out the assignment, one often
discovers that their performance was significantly different
from the instructions. If this is not uncovered, the therapist
may be misled and the patient can discount the therapist's advice as unhelpful and thus diminish his maneuverability. If, on
the other hand, it is made clear that the patient failed to follow
instructions, therapist maneuverability is maintained and, indeed, heightened, since the patient is now under more pressure
to follow advice accurately.

One-Downsmanship. Success in treatment depends greatly on the ability of the therapist to obtain strategic information
from the client and to elicit his compliance in carrying out suggestions or tasks. Some patients may respond to a position of
authority or expertise; if so, this stance can be useful. In our experience, however, compliance usually is reduced markedly if
the therapist is seen at the outset in a one-up or powerful position. Such a position intimidates many patients, who may already be embarrassed by their problems; and they are less likely
to reveal information that, in their view, will demean them even
further. Also, many patients interpret such a stance as a sign of
special wisdom or knowingness on the part of the therapist.
Thus, they may not give some information, or not give it clearly, on the assumption that the "perceptive" therapist will understand anyhow. Similar considerations arise when patients are
asked to accept ideas or suggestions.

It is often thought that a therapist who exudes expertness
inspires confidence in the patient and thereby overcomes his reluctance to cooperate. We assume, however, that the patient is
already motivated by his desire to be relieved from the distress
of his problem and is prepared to cooperate unless the therapist
interferes—for instance, by conveying to the patient that he has
failed in not seeing the appropriate solution already; that any
cooperation will be regarded as following orders; and that his
cooperation is in the therapist's interest and not necessarily his
own. Obviously, no therapist wants to convey any of these
things, but he risks doing so if he takes a one-up position. Such
a position can be conveyed by the therapist's comments ("I've

seen many cases like yours" or "I can't impress on you enough how important it is that you . . ."). It can also be conveyed by the self-conscious attempt to be "empathic" ("Yes, I can see your pain as you talk about that"). Usually, however, a one-up position is conveyed more subtly, so that in actual practice it is hard to know when one is taking such a position. Quite commonly, in the course of their training, therapists automatically come to adopt a one-up style. They no longer talk or act like people having a conversation; instead, there is the thoughtful and meaningful pause before making a comment, the knowing nod accompanied by the dramatic "Mmm, tell me more about that," the impersonal calmness in the face of the patient's anger, and so on.

The therapist-patient relationship inherently implies a position of presumed power. Therefore, taking a one-down position requires some doing, based not on the assumption that one-downness is especially influential but, simply that it is the surest way of avoiding a one-up position and of nullifying the patient's inclination toward seeing the therapist in that position. Patients, of course, will not necessarily be cooperative simply because one avoids the one-up stance; a one-down position, however, at least will not interfere with those patients who are ready to cooperate. For patients who still express resistance, the therapist must attempt to use this resistance to expedite cooperation (a matter dealt with in Chapter Five).

Although we have emphasized taking a one-down position, we do not mean that a one-up position is always to be avoided. As with all therapist positions and interventions, these are to be adapted to the specific client and specific situation in the course of treatment. Should one be working with a client whose cooperation would be enhanced by a therapist position of confidence and encouragement, then such a position would be appropriate. We have stressed the importance of one-downness for two reasons: In our experience, it is rather rare to find a client responsive to authority, and if it is not clear at the outset which position would be best, it is easier to shift from one-down to one-up than the converse. Therefore, the one-down position enables the therapist to be more maneuverable.

Individual and Conjoint Sessions. Although our approach is interactional, most of our treatment sessions are held with individuals or with two or three selected persons, rather than conjointly with the whole family. This is done for strategic and tactical reasons. Observers of our work have commented that they had thought we were family or systems oriented and were confused after seeing few or no conjoint sessions. We have had to explain that a systems approach primarily involves a *conceptual* framework; what matters is how one *views* problems, not whether one conducts a session with an individual or with two or more members of a family. For instance, there are "family therapists" who mainly hold conjoint sessions but conceive the problem in monadic terms, seeing the family members as a group of individuals rather than an interactional unit. Thus, although they hold conjoint sessions, the therapy is basically individual treatment.

We ourselves are principally concerned with the interaction revolving around the complaint, keeping in mind that ultimately we hope to interdict the problem-maintaining behavior of the participants. Consistent with that interactional view, we assume that alteration of the behavior of one member of an interactional unit—a family or some other group—can influence the behavior of other members of that unit. For the most part, we view problem-maintaining interactions as exemplifying a positive feedback or deviation-amplifying loop (Maruyama, 1963; Wender, 1968). That is, the identified patient's behavior invites solution-attempting behavior on the part of another, but that behavior escalates the identified patient's deviant behavior, which, in turn, invites stronger efforts, and so on. Seen as a loop, this cycle can be interrupted if the input of either or both participants is altered.

An analogy might be useful at this point: If one regarded an observed tennis rally as an undesirable interaction and therefore wished to end it as rapidly as possible, it would only require that *one* player not return the ball. The intervener's effectiveness would be reduced if he were limited to influencing only one particular player, especially if that player was less interested in ending the rally. However, his effectiveness would also be reduced if he were required to get *both* players to lay down their racquets simultaneously. Obviously, his maneuverability and effectiveness would be enhanced if he had the option to decide whether one or both players needed to be influenced and, if only one player, which of the two could more easily be influenced to lay down his racquet. For us, then, an important question is "Who in the family is most interested in resolving the problem?" It is likely to be the person most discomforted by the problem—that is, the chief complainant. Often—for instance, in child-centered problems—the complainant is not the identified patient. Most parents registering complaints are expecting or urging the therapist to treat the child. Others may encourage the therapist to see the whole family. With few exceptions, we will instead be planning to work primarily with one or both parents—although, for purposes of initial information gathering or for an intervention requiring a conjoint setting, we may schedule some conjoint sessions with the child and his parents, or an individual session with the child.

Individual sessions also can increase the therapist's maneuverability when two or more members of the family are truly bothered by a problem, are nearly equally interested in its resolution, but are in distinct conflict with each other. If the conflicting parties—for instance, a married couple—fight with each other in the sessions, the therapist's maneuverability is hampered, since he has to contend with management problems in the session itself. Similarly, in conjoint sessions with an adolescent and his parents, the teenager often becomes belligerent with his parents or, conversely, sits sullenly and refuses to say anything. These are such common occurrences that, as a general rule, we rarely meet conjointly with family members who are in significant conflict with each other. The therapist's maneuverability is made much greater if he meets with them separately.

Moreover, since the therapist wants the cooperation of the various members of a family, he must, in conjoint sessions, be careful not to take sides when they disagree, especially when the disagreement is strong and bitter. This effort will significantly limit what he can say and the range of rationales he can offer to the clients in gaining their cooperation. Additionally, he might want to suggest that one of the parties take a certain action; clearly, that action will have a different effect on the other parties if it has been discussed and deliberately planned in a joint session instead of appearing to be spontaneous. These limitations can be avoided and the therapist's options enhanced if he is free to work with the contending parties separately. After all, we are all more likely to cooperate with someone who commiserates with us, and the therapist is freer to commiserate with each person if seen separately. This option is closed to him if he is committed only to conjoint sessions.

In brief, when clients are seen separately, the therapist has the freedom to engage in an open coalition with each person and can more easily enlist each person's cooperation. Trainees have raised a legitimate question about this: "What if a couple compare notes between sessions? Won't that expose the therapist's inconsistency?" While there is some risk of that occurring, we believe it is a small one. First, such sessions usually are conducted with people who are in significant conflict with each other. Thus, if any comparison of "The therapist says I'm right" occurs, it is likely to be discounted by each party as simply the other's misinterpretation of the therapist's position. Second, there is little chance of such "comparing of notes" to arise. The therapist does not simply commiserate but follows that with some assignment which conceals the "coalition." However, such mutual confrontation can occur, and if one or the other party tries to confirm with the therapist exactly what he did say to the other spouse, the therapist can always fall back on the statement: "I can't control how people interpret what I say after they leave my office." The questioning party is likely to then discount the other spouse's report. As an alternative, the therapist can see both "warring parties" together, confess to double-talk, and explain that he felt forced to wheedle them both because they are so stubbornly locked into their vendetta that he could see no other reasonable way to get them to take any action necessary for the ending of their struggle. Thus, his honest admission still can be used to apply pressure on them to cooperate with suggestions.

Tactics with Difficult Patients

Two major categories of patients most frequently present serious obstacles to the therapist's maneuverability, if not to treatment itself: (1) patients who enter treatment under duress and (2) patients who attempt to impose impossible restrictions on the therapy. For these two categories, we are using the term "difficult patient." By "difficult patient" we are not referring to those common obstacles many patients present which can slow treatment down—for example, being vague or argumentative or passive. The "difficult patient," as we are using the term here, threatens to prevent therapy from getting under way at all.

The "Window Shopper." Most patients come in to see a therapist because they are truly distressed by some circumstances within themselves or with another person, and are looking for help from the therapist for that distress. However, a number of other "patients" come in primarily at the behest of another person and are therefore in the office under duress or coercion. Such a patient may state a complaint, but as he elaborates on it or is asked to explain why he sought treatment at the time he did, it becomes clear that he is not particularly bothered by what he complains of but that someone else is. The someone else is usually the person who has pushed him into treatment. Thus, this kind of patient is not personally interested in making any change in the complaint; and if this fact is not recognized, many hours of effort can be wasted in a treatment that has never really begun.

We have used the term "window shopper" for this kind of individual, since it is an everyday and succinct analogy for characterizing this position. A good salesman knows he is not going to make a sale with every customer who enters his shop. But he also knows that he will almost never make a sale to someone who has come into the store just to get out of the rain. As a face-saving gesture, such persons may attempt to act like interested customers, but their eyes are on the rain and they are simply waiting for it to let up. They are not in the store because of any interest in a possible purchase but under the "duress" of the weather. They are not truly customers but obscure this by acting as if they were. Similarly, the patients to whom this section refers are not in treatment to make any change in the stated complaint but are there under some coercion.

Examples of this kind of patient are the teenager dragged in by his parents, the "wayward" husband coming in at the urging of his wife, and the offender ordered by the court. Another common example is the patient who presents some complaint but whose hidden agenda is to get the therapist to confirm that he is disabled and entitled to some form of disability payment: "I've got this chest pain which has kept me out of work for the past six months, and the company doctor feels I need to see you."

The principal error that therapists make in this situation is to embark on treatment as if the patient is ready to get down to business but is simply having trouble doing so. This error is likely to occur if the therapist either fails to check for any coercive element in the client's motivation, or ignores it if it is presented, or is too intent on finding out more about the problem and other data and fails to notice whether the patient is much *bothered* by the problem.

If the therapist does recognize that the client is in the office only under duress, he need not throw up his hands and terminate the case. Instead, he can use certain tactics that may get treatment under way and, ultimately, achieve a good outcome.

First of all, he can *renegotiate the contract.* In our experience, a few patients who enter therapy under duress do want to make some change in a complaint, but it is not the complaint they first stated when asked "What's the problem?" As a first step, then, the patient can be offered the opportunity to register such a complaint, which then can become the explicit or implied focus of any therapeutic effort:

Th: OK. So if I hear you right, your wife is making a big fuss about your drinking, but as far as you are concerned it's really no problem. And if it weren't for the flap she is making, you probably wouldn't . . .

Pt: Yeah, I think she meant business about seeing the attorney.

Th: ... be here, at least at this time. Well, all right, I can follow your being rattled about that, but I'd feel funny working with you on something which is no problem to you. I'd rather spend my time working on something that is meaningful to you, not just to Dorothy. So let me ask you this: Is there any other kind of problem you've been struggling with which really does bother you; maybe something which you have had in mind doing something about but always put off?

Pt: It's funny you should ask that. You see ... Well, I don't know if this is the kind of thing you work with. Oh, hell. I might as well say it. I've been stalemated in my job for a number of years now. No promotions; my assignments more and more routine; some juicy contracts given to guys I know can't do the job on them I can. And yet, dammit, I'm in the dark as to why this is happening, and I don't know what to do about it.

Th: And this bugs you a lot more than your drinking?

Pt: Oh, yeah. Do you work on that kind of problem?

The client has offered a "renegotiated contract." He is not interested in working on drinking, but he is interested in doing something about his work situation. He is, thus, no longer a "window shopper" but a "customer." The therapist is not committed to working on that new problem or, certainly, to working on *only* that problem. He might, for example, decide in the course of treatment to intervene in the drinking problem by using the work problem as a context for such an intervention. We are, therefore, not using "renegotiating the contract" in the more customary sense of making the focus and goal of treatment completely explicit and agreed upon with the client. Rather, we are using it in the sense of offering the "window shopper" an opportunity to come forth with a different complaint, which he is interested in changing.

If the client fails to come up with a problem he wishes to work on, the therapist can suggest an alternate problem. He can, for instance, introduce a rather incontrovertible problem—the fact that the client is there because someone is on his back to seek treatment. Aside from family members coerced into treatment by other family members—spouse or parents—this challenge can be appealing to offenders coerced into treatment by the court and the probation officer:

Th: OK. You don't feel you really have any problem that is bothering you or that needs any treatment. But you do have one problem.

Pt: What's that?

Th: Well, you have a probation officer on your back. He's the one who is making it his business to see that you come in here, and he's not likely to just let it go at one session.

Pt: Yeah, that's true.

Th: All right. You may not be interested in working on what your P.O. or the court thinks is important, but would you be interested in getting your P.O. off your back?

Pt: Hell, yes. I'd be interested in that.

If the patient agrees to this "contract," it does not mean that the therapist is restricted or even committed to that goal. In any case, the probation officer is likely to "get off his back" if the probationer is conducting his life in a way that allows his officer to feel more relaxed and trusting of him. He may, for instance, have to do something about his difficulties in employment, in socializing, perhaps in the marital arena; and all these areas are part of therapy.

A second level of intervention—the one that we have used most often and found most effective—involves *working with the complainant.* A significant element in our overall view of problems is that, with little exception, the problem is maintained and escalated by particular *interactions* between the identified patient and others caught up in the problem. Those interactions are, primarily, efforts that are made to resolve the problem but that, instead, maintain the problem. Thus, it is not only the identified patient who may make such "problem-solving" attempts but also others. If another person is more discomfited by the identified patient's problem than the patient himself is, that other person is likely to be the one making the most effort to solve the problem. Such a person, then, is the real complainant; and the therapist can shift to working with him rather than with the identified patient. The complainant is usually the person placing the identified patient under duress to enter treatment.

Th: If I hear you right, the only thing that is really bothering you is the flap Dorothy is making about your drinking and . . .

Pt: Yeah, she really makes a federal case out of it.

Th: . . . other than that, everything would be all right.

Pt: Yeah. Right. I wish she would get off my back about it.

Th: Well, I'd feel funny about wasting our time on something that's no real problem to you. It would be a waste of time for both of us. If she's making a big fuss over a small matter, then the only thing that would seem to make sense is if I could see her and maybe help her to relax a bit more about your drinking. Would you be interested in that?

Pt: Oh, yeah. That could make a big difference.

The therapist would then call the wife, set up an appointment to see her alone, and begin with her as with any case: "What's the problem? How have you been trying to deal with it? What minimal goal of treatment would suffice?" Since the wife is likely to view the husband as the one who needs to see the therapist, some framing on the phone and at the beginning of the appointment will be necessary, so that she accepts being asked in as a logical request. There is also an enormous advantage if this framing indicates that the therapist may want to see her more than once: "Could you meet with me, at least once, to help me see the real extent of your husband's problem more clearly?"

A third tactic is to *get the "window shopper" down to business.* In a few cases (for example, in cases where the complainant is a probation officer or a judge), it may be difficult or infeasible to call in the complainant. If the identified patient in such cases does not offer a "renegotiated" problem, then the therapist can attempt to get him interested in the treatment. If this can be accomplished, it will *not* be done by exhorting him to take his problem seriously, to buckle down to treatment, and the like. This is the one pitfall to avoid. The therapist has some chance of success, however, if he applies a different pressure by going the other way—by taking the position with the "client" that treatment probably is inadvisable. The identified patient now has the opportunity to convince the therapist why it could be in his own best interest to do something about *his* problem. The therapist can apply additional pressure by extending his position of "Why bother?"—perhaps by offering reasons for avoiding treatment that are likely to be aversive to the "window shopper." For example, if the identified patient has indicated that he sees himself as a benevolent, nonpunitive individual, the therapist can redefine his problem as a clever and powerful weapon, a weapon that he should not give up through treatment but instead should use against some particular person: "What you have been doing, whether you recognize it or not, is a beautiful way of getting revenge on your spouse, and, God knows, you are entitled to revenge." Conversely, if a "window shopper" has strongly expressed anger toward another person, the therapist can suggest that the other person would be disadvantaged if the client were to solve his problem: "No, I don't think you should do anything about your problem. You see, if you became more accepting, that would put [the other person] in a one-down position to you, and I am rather certain he would become upset by this."

If none of the above interventions are feasible or successful, then there is no point in trying to keep the client in treatment. Such treatment would be time wasting and frustrating and possibly worse, since the client can later convince others that he tried treatment but it failed to help. Thus, termination is the appropriate move. This still leaves the question of *how* one terminates. For example, if the therapist simply says that he does not believe the client is serious enough about his problem to make treatment worthwhile, the client can go to another therapist and start his "game" all over. Instead, the therapist might present the client with a challenging prediction: "Well, you're saying you might give treatment a try. But I know and you know you're not ready to do a damn thing about your problem. I think the best thing for you is to go through the motions of treatment but not let any therapist get anywhere with you. Just keep them trying. Now, I suppose I could let you do that with me but I don't like wasting my time baby-sitting, so I won't be setting up any further appointment with you. Besides, there are any number of therapists around who don't mind that kind of thing. You can pooh-pooh what I'm saying, but you don't have to take my word for it. I don't care who you see, you'll prove I'm right."

The Restrictive Patient. Certain clients threaten to sabotage treatment from the outset, usually by attempting to set conditions of treatment, which, if accepted, would limit the therapist's freedom to maneuver constructively. They are not necessarily attempting this wittingly; usually this difficulty appears to arise from some fixed belief about an absolutely necessary condition of treatment.

In this next example, the patient attempts to control the focus of treatment after becoming angered at the therapist's suggestions that he make some changes with his girl friend, the focus of the client's presenting complaint.

Pt: I have a difficulty in feeling rapport with you. I came back because I have an earnestness of intent, in terms of my own growth, that requires that I stick in there—hang in there. And I know that if I'm pissed at you, it's really some component of me that I'm pissed at. And yet I am seriously concerned about my ability to work with you in terms of the resolution of the problem that I came in with. There are other things that are coming up for me, in terms of working with you, that are of interest to me, and I imagine that one day I'll lay them to rest. Before, certainly, I could ever be enlightened, I would need to lay them to rest. And I'm willing to pursue them now in the series of five sessions with you, and I'm concerned that I'm not dealing with what I most want to deal with, which is this relationship—which is a nonrelationship, sort of, right now—with the woman that I'm interested in dating. So I could go ahead and give you more data, more information, and that, it seems to

me, isn't going to allay—that's not going to allay my concern of a
lack of rapport or understanding, something like that. And I
don't know what that comes from—what it would take to establish that rapport. And so my thoughts in the matter are I'm per-
fectly willing and happy and delighted to continue to work with
you in terms of that issue that I just defined—rapport—or my
anger toward you, which I interpret as anger toward me, or sixteen other things that might come up, and I would be willing to
do that only if my primary reason for coming here is being
taken care of in a way that I feel comfortable with.

This sort of difficulty may occur especially with patients
who have had extensive prior treatment and are trying to impose similar conditions on the present treatment—despite the
clear implication that such treatment did not succeed. ("My
previous therapist encouraged me to scream and throw things
when I felt angry.") Others, while genuinely looking for help,
resent some of the inconveniences that treatment may entail. In
any case, the conditions proposed by such patients, explicitly or
implicitly, must be dealt with effectively; otherwise, they will
tie the therapist's hands and make any beneficial outcome of
treatment most unlikely. These restricting conditions fall into a
few categories—restricting the therapist's freedom to comment,
to set appointments and pace treatment, and to see others involved in the family or in the problem system—but since they
may pose serious obstacles, we will here consider some ways of
intervening with them effectively.

Some patients can seriously jeopardize therapy by asking
the therapist to enter into a conspiracy of silence against another member of the family, usually the spouse. For example,
when the therapist has either seen the spouse or is planning to
as part of treatment, the restrictive patient may announce that
he would like to reveal something to the therapist, but with the
promise that it not be conveyed to the spouse. In such an instance, the therapist should interrupt before the "revelation"
and make clear that he needs to see the spouse without constraints:

Th: Before you tell me whatever you had in mind, I need to make something clear. If I'm to be of any help in resolving the problem, I need to be free to take up with you or your spouse whatever I judge is relevant to resolving the problem. When she comes in, I will be informing her of the same thing. Therefore, if you want to go ahead and bring up what you were going to, it would be with the understanding that I might take it up with her, but only if I feel it is important to do so. If you can't allow me that freedom, then it would be better not to tell me, at least until you've had some time to think it over.

On a few occasions, the client may have already revealed something but asks that, in anticipation of the spouse's visit, it be kept from her. In that case, the therapist can still ask that he be free to decide whether to bring it up or not. However, should the patient insist on the therapist's collusion by silence, there are two other possible courses. First, the therapist can tell the patient that the advantages of seeing the spouse would be outweighed by the onus of a conspiracy of silence and that he will therefore not see the spouse until the patient has had a chance to think it over. An alternative is to suggest a compromise with the patient: "I will go ahead and see your wife, and I will not reveal to her what you have told me. I will simply say that there is something you've told me which I will not be relaying to her; that if she is to know about it, it will have to come from you directly."

Conceivably, there are other ways of intervening in this kind of threatened restrictiveness; the main thing to avoid is agreeing to the conspiracy of silence.

Other patients will attempt to restrict the therapist's option to see family members when their involvement could be central to the resolution of the problem. Most commonly, this attempted restriction arises when a patient has complained about her spouse but then refuses to give permission to her therapist to see the spouse. Instead of accepting that refusal and continuing with the treatment, or lengthily questioning the patient's motivation for the refusal, or urging her to give approval, the therapist can simply acknowledge the patient's wish. He can comment that the refusal is legitimate but that the spouse's participation is important; consequently, the patient is setting herself difficult odds if she wants to resolve the problem: "However, Rome wasn't built in a day, so there's no rush. We'll just struggle along as best we can without your husband's participation." The pressure is then on the patient—all the more if treatment, as predicted, meanders unproductively. Additional opportunities for useful pressure can occur. For example, in response to almost any reference the client makes to her husband, the therapist can suggest that that agenda be tabled, since "Without having seen your husband, I don't really know what I could do with that." Sessions can also be spaced further apart, with the rationale that "Your strong resistance to having your husband come in might be a valid indication that you should not resolve your problem too quickly. Your unconscious may be telling us something we should pay serious attention to." If all else fails, then the threat of termination may need to be made.

A more serious restriction arises when a patient attempts to intimidate the therapist by explosive anger in response to comments or questions raised by his therapist. If the explosiveness is questioned, the patient usually defends it on the basis that the fullest expression of his feelings is not only legitimate in treatment but necessary for dealing with his problem. If the therapist accepts this reasoning, he will find himself becoming more and more careful, fearing that the "wrong" question or comment will bring forth an unsettling attack. Obviously, treatment cannot proceed in a constructive way under such conditions. The therapist must convey to the patient that such intimidation must stop or treatment will be terminated. He could simply say, "If you continue to intimidate me with your outbursts of explosive anger, I will have to terminate treatment." But the patient does not feel that he is trying to intimidate the therapist. Instead, he believes that he is legitimately expressing himself and therefore views the therapist's comments as a form of harassment. ("Why are you always so critical of me?") Thus, to put an ultimatum directly invites yet another howl of outrage. This can be circumvented and the patient's compliance enhanced if the ultimatum can be put in a "one-down" manner: "There is something you need to know about me, and I think it important because I might not be the appropriate therapist for you. I know that expressing feelings is important, and I try to allow for that with all my patients. However, I am sadly limited in being unable to handle much intensity in those expressions. So, when you raise your voice and shout, it goes beyond my level of handling it. Unfortunately, the only thing that happens then is that I get paralyzed, and when I am paralyzed I am no good to anyone. If, in expressing your feelings, it is very important to express them that intensely, then it would be a waste of your time and money to work with a therapist who just gets paralyzed. However, if you want to work with me, then it would have to be with the understanding that expressions of feelings will have to be conveyed with less emotion. I know it's unfortunate, but that's the way I am."

The following example is another variation of putting the patient on notice about the expression of anger; the therapist uses a one-down position to accomplish this:

Pt: [My previous therapist] kept talking about giving up the anger because he found it detrimental to his practice. I mean, he said, "You know, at times your anger is so overwhelming I can't do anything—I can't think clearly. I'm thinking here, maybe I've got to defend myself."

Th: Let me address that point because that's the last thing I wanted to bring up with you before we move on to something else. Last week you said, "Well, I'm angry, but I'm not angry today." *I* experienced the anger, and I found myself . . . You know, maybe I didn't look it, but I was kind of cringing inside. And when I reacted that way, I started handling you with kid gloves, like fragile china. And my colleagues pointed out that, in a sense, if I do that, I'm giving you the shaft.

Pt: No, I agree with that also, and so the only way I can . . .

Th: Because if I do that, I'm not getting down to the things I need to get down to. So I've decided that I probably want to err on the side of coming on too strong, rather than allowing that feeling to take hold and being too passive and handling you too gingerly. Is that all right with you?

Pt: Yes, I can agree with that.

There is one other type of restriction by intimidation, and it can be a most paralyzing one. It is the threat of physical assault. This threat, which is all the more intimidating because it is implicit, is most likely to be encountered with people labeled as "paranoid." The patient does not make open threats; instead, he will, without explanation, become visibly agitated, rise from his chair, pace about, and pound his fist on a wall or table. Others may, more quietly and chillingly, make veiled threats: "You know what I feel like doing right now?" If these threats come after the therapist has made some comment, he is likely to become quite fearful and therefore careful in almost anything he might say or do. The tension can also interfere with his judgment in other ways. This situation thus is therapeutically untenable and, moreover, potentially dangerous. The therapist must intervene to establish an unintimidating context of treatment.

As with the angry patient, the patient needs to be informed that any continuation of intimidating threats will result in termination. Here, however, the fact that the threats are intimidating needs to be made explicit. We believe the commonest mistake is for the therapist to conceal his intimidation. If the threatening patient is deliberately trying to terrorize the therapist, he will regard the therapist's avoidance of the subject, the studied failure to acknowledge intimidation, as proof of his success. If, on the other hand, the patient's threats are the result of a passive defensive posture (so that he is fighting not like a lion but like a cornered animal), he is likely to continue, since he interprets the therapist's quietness as disapproval or withdrawal. In either case, there is much less error to be made if the therapist quietly but firmly acknowledges that he is feeling intimidated by those actions of the patient: "The truth is you scare the hell out of me when you stare at me and snort or suddenly get up out of your chair and go pacing around. And I can't think straight when I'm scared. And if I can't think straight, I can't be of any use to you. I know it may sound funny, but if

I'm going to be of any help to you, you're going to have to help me out too." Depending on the patient's response, it can be left at that; or, if need be, the threat to terminate treatment will have to be made more explicit.

We have discussed these four types of restrictions patients may attempt to impose on the therapist since they constitute the most frequent and potentially disruptive ones. Other kinds may also ocur; they can be dealt with in similar ways.

❦ 3 ❦

Setting the Stage
for Treatment

Therapy usually is not considered to have begun until the patient comes in for the initial interview, or even later if initial diagnostic sessions are considered separate from treatment itself. The transactions that occur in the setting up of that first interview are regarded, for the most part, as routine necessities. In our view, however, all contacts with clients may affect treatment; therefore, if one intends to do therapy efficiently, planning is necessary at all stages of treatment. One of those stages occurs before the client has come in. With few exceptions, this stage involves telephone contact when patients call for appointments or information regarding treatment. These contacts may not play an important part in all cases. In certain situations, however, a caller makes a request or attempts to impose a precondition on treatment, which, if acceded to, could create significant difficulty in the initial session or later in therapy. In this chapter, we describe these situations and indicate how they can be handled.

Appointments for a Third Party

One person may call to propose an appointment for another. For example, a father may call about his son: "We are having a lot of trouble with our fifteen-year-old son, and he has finally agreed he needs help. I understand you work with teenagers, so I am calling to arrange an appointment for him. We really feel he needs to talk with someone because he can't talk with us." In making this call, and in his brief comments, the father is clearly indicating that he regards his son as the identified patient but that he and presumably his wife are more discomforted by their son's problem than the son is; in that sense, they are the complainants. As a safe rule of thumb, whoever in a system is most discomforted by a problem is the one most committed to seeking change. Correspondingly, the complainant is also the one best worked with in treatment.

In the above example, a number of difficulties probably will arise if the therapist simply accedes to the father's request and sets up an appointment with the son. Since the son's motivation is questionable at best, he is likely not to show up for the appointment; or, if he does show up, the chances are that he will not be cooperative. In any case, treatment will have begun on the implicit understanding that the boy will be treated while the parents will wait passively for him to be "cured," much as one turns in a defective television set and picks it up from the repairman after it is fixed. It is true that the therapist could call in the parents later in treatment, but to do so at that time and in that order is more risky. The parents would have been allowed to view the problem and treatment as something separate from themselves; and they could now view invitations to participate a failure on the therapist's part to "reach" their son.

Instead of acceding and thereby reducing his options in further treatment, the therapist can offer the father an alternative:

Th: Yes, I do work with teenage problems, but before I set up an appointment, let me first ask: How interested is your son in seeing a psychotherapist?

F: Well, we've been encouraging it for some time now, and he has resisted until last night. We had a big blowup and then a long talk, but I feel we finally got through to him. He said if we called he might be willing to see someone.

Th: OK. Since he is rather questionably motivated, I think a lot of time could be saved in the long run if I could have a chance to meet with you and your wife, at least for the first session. Partly, I could get some needed background about your son; but even more, I might be able to explore some avenue to motivate him better, not only to come in but to make the best use of any sessions.

If the father agrees to this proposal, the therapist will be able to start treatment off on a very different footing and one with more likelihood of success. The parents will have agreed implicitly that they are initiating treatment, that they are consulting a therapist about their son and are taking an active role in that treatment. At the same time, this confirms their authoritative position in the family. Finally, it will make it easier to have them come in for subsequent sessions.

What might the therapist do if the father demurs from this proposal? ("I can understand your wanting to talk with my wife and me, but we really feel the need to strike while the iron is hot. It has taken us so long to get even this concession from him that we are afraid if we don't seize this opportunity we won't be able to get him in.") In such a case, the therapist need not stand on ceremony by insisting that they come in without the boy. He can appear to acquiesce while accomplishing the same end: "All right, that might be best. Have him come in with you, then. It might add something if I could sit down with all of you this first time. However, since you indicated that his motivation is shaky, don't be dismayed if he refuses at the last minute. If he does, don't make an issue of his coming in, but you and your wife come ahead without him. He may need to know you are serious in your concern, as shown by your opening the door to treatment." In either case, treatment will still be initiated with the same framing—they will be coming in without him, as originally proposed, or they will come in with him as concerned parents.

What if the father is adamant that the son be seen alone? ("No. He really needs to talk to someone, to unburden himself. Our presence would only interfere with that. We might come in later if you really felt it necessary.") Again, the therapist need not stand on ceremony. One basic aspect of maneuverability is to take one's time; not everything need be resolved right away, and time is on the therapist's side. He can graciously accede to the father's demand but then put the onus for the outcome of that venture on the father: "All right. I understand your feelings about it, and I will be glad to make an appointment for him. However, you are entitled to know that when a boy is as questionably motivated as I gather your son is, it rarely works out well to start off this way. But I will trust your judgment and hope that he does utilize this opportunity for help, and if he does, fine. But if I recognize that he is just going through the motions and only wasting his time and your money, then I would be delinquent in not letting you know that, and in that case it would be necessary for me to meet with you and your wife. Anyhow, there's no need to worry about that now. Let me meet with him and see how it goes." Should the son, surprisingly, turn out to be cooperative with treatment, fine. If, as is more likely, he is resistant to it, the therapist is in a maneuverable and influential position, since the son will have proved him right and he can more credibly enlist the parents' cooperation.

These examples highlight one facet of pretreatment issues: Who should be seen in a first interview, especially when the caller is not the identified patient? What is described above can be applied to a parent calling for a child, grown children calling for an elderly parent, or one spouse calling for another. There are exceptions to this rule, although they are rare: a spouse calling for the other but at the other's behest and simply for convenience. ("My husband asked me to set up an appointment for next week. He would have called, but he unexpectedly had to be out of town this week.")

Information from a Previous Therapist

A caller may say that she would like to make an appointment and may then suggest that the therapist contact her previous therapist for information regarding her prior treatment; she may further suggest that the information be obtained and reviewed *before* the first visit: "I've been in treatment with Dr. X for three years, but I recently moved here and feel I need to continue therapy. I wonder if I can see you, but I think you should contact Dr. X and get his records of my care before I come in. He knows me so well that I think it would help you to understand my problem if you could have that information first." In making this suggestion, the patient is entertaining certain assumptions: that therapy with the new therapist will simply be a continuation of previous treatment, and that both therapists work alike and share the same views.

If the therapist simply accedes to her request, he may be confirming these assumptions, and treatment can begin on a problematic note. First of all, the therapist will have implicitly aligned himself with the previous therapist by using his records to learn about her. Should it turn out that she has harbored some resentment toward that therapist, a resentment not apparent in the initial phone call, it will be much more difficult for the new therapist to dissociate himself later on. Acceding to her request also implies that "understanding" her can come from others, perhaps better than from herself. This can invite her to take a passive role in treatment, and she is under less obligation to make herself plain to the current therapist: "Didn't Dr. X explain that to you? I don't see why we have to go over it all again." Finally, it leaves the patient less prepared for differences in approach between her previous and current therapists: "I know I'm supposed to bring in my dreams." Yet such differences are likely indicated, since her problem had not been resolved after three years of treatment.

A therapist can avoid these potential pitfalls by offering a different opening to treatment: "I would like to get Dr. X's views on your previous treatment, and that could be useful. However, I have found I can make better use of that kind of information if I first sit down with the patient and get a fresh view on some basic data regarding the problem. Then, *after that*, I would be glad to get Dr. X's observations and thoughts."

Doing Therapy on the Phone

Patients who have been in prior treatment—especially, in treatment emphasizing therapist rapport and "support"—may try to initiate a therapy session during their call for an appointment:

Pt: If you are accepting new patients, I'd like to make an appointment. Dr. X referred me to you and spoke most highly of you. I don't know how much information you want right now, but there are a few things you should know. I've been having episodes of depression since high school but didn't learn till later that they were expressions of my hostility toward men. And, you see, that's the trouble because my husband is very domineering, and I'm worried that I will slip back into depression if I can't work this thing out. I know I must be near the edge of depression; my weight has been going up, and recently they discovered my blood pressure was high. Is it possible that I could be doing this, unconsciously, because of some resentment toward Dr. Y? He's my internist and, of course, an authority figure.

Here the patient is inviting the therapist to comment about her narrative. Since she is being so scattered and vague, he could be tempted to ask her to clarify what she has been saying, or he could simply ask her what the main problem is right now. He might even try to make a comment about her last question— for example, that her speculation may be correct. But to respond to this material is to imply that the telephone is a legitimate medium for conducting psychotherapy, when the initial purpose of the call was to set up an appointment. Such a response tends to frame therapy as a matter of casual discussion, which can be conducted impersonally, and as a transaction in which the patient can determine the timing and pacing of sessions merely by picking up the phone. Rather, the patient should be viewing treatment as a task-oriented getting down to business, in which the appropriate pacing and timing are to be determined primarily by the therapist.

We do not consider this kind of invitation as necessarily manipulative on the patient's part but more as an outcome of previous treatment, in which the patient had been trained to rely on discussions with her therapist regardless of the time of day or night. Such a patient, in our view, needs help in readjusting to different roles and functions of patient and therapist in treatment. Here the therapist should make clear to the caller that treatment sessions are separate from life outside the consulting room, that therapy is a getting together to conduct the business of problem solving, and that for both patient and therapist it is an active process, not just general "rapping." All this can be conveyed as follows:

Th: [Politely but firmly] Let me interrupt. What you are telling me may be quite important. The trouble is that I have difficulty digesting important and complex information over the phone, and I would not be able to do justice to it. Let me suggest that you go ahead and set up an appointment, and then, when you come in, I can give that information the attention it deserves.

Handling matters this way can save considerable time on such a phone call and also prepares the patient not to attempt to use the phone to conduct therapy at any subsequent time.

Requests for Family Counseling

Since family therapy has grown to a sizable movement and entered public awareness, therapists may get calls proposing a meeting with the entire family of the caller—either because a referring source has recommended "family therapy" or because the caller himself believes that family counseling is required. A father, for instance, may say: "Our family has been having a lot of trouble, and I think we all need to come in for counseling. Mainly, we need to learn to communicate better, so I was wondering if we could set up an appointment."

If the therapist agrees to a family session, significant problems can result. First of all, he thereby implicitly legiti-

mizes conjoint family therapy as the appropriate approach for
problem resolution and consequently reduces his maneuverability if he feels that some other modality is indicated. Second,
such a session can waste time, since input from all family members may prove unnecessary. The therapist also may have difficulty in eliciting the problem or complaint, not only because of
the varied inputs by a number of people but because the conjoint family format narrows the legitimate focus of treatment to
what the *family at large* may consider to be the problem. For
example, it can be much more difficult for the caller to say
what, specifically, bothers him, and he is more constrained to
state a complaint in general terms of "we": "We don't communicate as a family" or "We don't have a sense of being a unified
family." Furthermore, if the caller's actual complaint is marital
—and, especially, if the marital difficulty is primarily sexual—a
family session can prove awkward and uninformative. Similarly,
if the complaint is about the behavior of one of the children,
the conjoint family context makes it more difficult for the father to say which child he is particularly concerned about and,
concretely, what about the child bothers him. After all, in a
family conference setting, many people feel that it is poor form
to blame any one person.

The therapist can avoid these difficulties by asking the father on the initial phone call, "What is the *main* problem that
you are concerned about?" If he responds vaguely, the question
can be put more pointedly: "Are you concerned primarily
about yourself or about your marriage or about one or more of
the kids?" If he mentions either of the first two areas, then the
therapist can suggest that only he and his wife come in, at least
in the first interview. If the complaint is about one or more of
the children, the therapist can suggest that either only he and his
wife come in or that they bring only the child or children they
have concern about.

We realize that this latter move runs counter to conventional family practice. However, in many conventional family
therapies, it is a basic premise that a child's symptoms are an expression of some basic flaw in the structure or organization of
the family unit, so that to exclude the other children is to iden-

tify the child as the patient rather than as the symptom bearer of the family. Since our own premises are different, our practice is different. First, we do not view a child's problematic behavior as necessarily or primarily a function of deeper problems in the family system but, rather, as an outcome of the parents' attempted solutions in trying to control or help him. We might also suspect, in such cases, that the calling of a family conference is one form of that "solution." Second, if the parents are concerned about—or bothered by—their child, it will be easier to deal with this effectively if it is made explicit rather than kept hidden or veiled. Thus, for us, it is not a matter of "fingering" the child by having only him brought in, but that he is already being "fingered" and it is better to have this overt than covert. Then, in the initial session with the parents, the therapist can obtain additional data to help him decide whom to see in the next session and how to frame the treatment to the parents so that he can maintain maneuverability in making decisions about subsequent sessions.

Requests for Specific Treatment

In other cases, patients may ask for specific treatment modalities: "I need hypnosis," or "I'm looking for long-term treatment," or "I will need medication," and so forth. In large measure, these requests can be handled similarly to the request for family counseling. Even if one uses a number of treatment modalities, such as hypnosis and medications, he still must set the stage for treatment in such a way that, from the beginning, he can maintain the maneuverability to exercise his best judgment during the progress of treatment. Thus, to the caller asking for hypnosis, the therapist can reply that he does use hypnosis but only when he feels that it offers the best approach for resolving a problem; that he cannot make that determination over the phone but only after face-to-face discussion. He thus emphasizes that his willingness to meet with the patient is not to be taken as an implied promise to use hypnosis.

If the caller requests a treatment approach that the therapist does not use—for instance, psychoanalytic therapy—then there is no point in hedging. It is better to say, "I'm sorry, but I don't use psychoanalysis in my work; if you are specifically looking for that kind of treatment, I can suggest names of people I know who do use it. If, however, you are mainly interested in resolving some problem, even though this may not involve or require analysis, then I would be willing to meet with you." If the caller is intent on analytic treatment, he will not go further with the therapist. But if he is not totally committed to it and is sufficiently interested in resolving a problem, then his decision to work with the therapist will be on the basis that the therapist is to guide the form and course of treatment.

Problems in Appointment Setting

Callers sometimes will attempt to set the time of their appointment in a restrictive way:

Caller: I'd like to make an appointment for myself, and I wonder if I could see you today.

Th: I'm sorry, but I'm all booked up today. Are you in a crisis?

Caller: No. It's an old problem. The trouble is that in my work I never know when I will be free until I get to work, and today I found I could be free so I was hoping I could get in.

Even if the therapist is willing to "squeeze" this caller in —at lunchtime or by extending his working hours—he will be acceding to an arrangement in which treatment timing and pacing are totally in the hands of the patient; more important, such an arrangement will not allow for any planning of treatment. The tasks of gaining needed data, of formulating the focus of treatment, of assigning homework, and of assessing the impact of that homework—all will be done on a hit-or-miss basis, since the therapist will never know how soon or how long it will be before the patient comes in again. It is not in the patient's best interest to embark on such a chancy venture. If the work constraints are as he says, he will be better off if he either learns to live with his problem or finds some way to rearrange his work schedule so that it will permit his planning on treatment. Work schedules are rarely as restrictive as this caller implies. More often, the individual is posing his own restrictions, which may be part of the very problem for which he is seeking help. Therefore, the therapist must make it clear that he will not begin treatment on the caller's proposed terms: "I'm sorry I can't oblige you today. Sometimes I'm able to see people on very short notice. You could call me again just in case I might have some time, but I think it only fair to tell you that you are setting up almost impossible odds if you are hoping to work on a problem while never being able to plan appointments ahead of time." Even if such a patient is seen, treatment will have started with the onus on the patient to find an alternative to his uncertain scheduling.

A variant of this problem occurs when a caller asks for an appointment but mentions that he can afford to come in only once a month. Here again, the therapist can tell the caller that, although some problems can be resolved with that kind of timetable, many others require more flexibility of scheduling. If the problem is a financial one, the caller can be offered an alternative: that he meet with the therapist for a specific number of sessions, probably in the range of five to ten meetings and on a weekly basis, and that treatment will stop at the end of that time even if the problem is not resolved. Should further treatment then be necessary, the patient would take a vacation from treatment for two or three months, after which he could recontract for another number of sessions, and so on. In our experience, many patients who raise obstacles of this kind are willing to pursue treatment on such a redefined basis.

Requests for Information

On occasion, a caller may indicate that he is seriously looking for help but wishes to get some information about the therapist and treatment first. Common questions are "Are you a psychologist, psychiatrist, or psychiatric social worker?" "How much do you charge?" "What is your approach to treatment, your main orientation?" "When is the latest [or earliest] in the

day I can get an appointment?" "Do you take insurance?" The
therapist has no way of knowing whether these questions are
being raised because the caller is ambivalent about treatment or
whether they are asked as legitimate points of information.
Therefore, although therapists of some orientations might feel
uncomfortable with such blunt practical questions, we would
give such a caller the benefit of the doubt, at least to begin
with, and answer his questions forthrightly and succinctly. If he
is simply asking for relevant information and he contracts to see
the therapist, treatment will have started on an advantageous
footing: the therapist's manner will have conveyed a useful note
of "getting down to business" in the exchange of information—
including sensitive information that the patient subsequently
will be asked to reveal about himself. If, in the call, it soon appears that the caller is not satisfied with the answers he has gotten and he goes on to further and less specific questions, then
the therapist can terminate the call as quickly and graciously as
he wants.

At the risk of being redundant, we now illustrate many of
the key points in this chapter by a transcribed tape recording of
two simulated phone contacts. In the first example, a wife is
calling for marital therapy, operating on the premise that her
husband must attend the first session, even if she has to "twist
his arm" to get him to the office:

Th: Hello.

Pt: Hello, is this Dr. French?

Th: Yes, this is Dr. French.

Pt: Hi. This is Mrs. Cooper calling. I was recommended by
some good friends of ours who saw you several years ago, and,
well, I just wanted to make sure—do you do marriage counseling?

Th: Yes, excuse me a second—could you speak up a little
louder? I didn't even get your name because there's some noise
outside my office.

Pt: Oh, my name is Mrs. Cooper, and I was recommended to you by some friends of mine who saw you a few years ago. Do you do marriage counseling?

Th: I work, you know, I work with marriage problems, but I'm not a marriage counselor; I'm a psychiatrist, so . . . I can explain that difference later, when we get together.

Pt: OK, but you do work on marital problems?

Th: Yes.

Pt: Well, my husband and I would like to make an appointment to come in and see you.

Th: Let me just ask something: How interested is your husband in coming in to see a counselor or a therapist?

Pt: Well, we had marriage counseling a few years ago, and it didn't work out very well. But that was just because my husband really didn't give it a chance, so he's not very anxious about coming in, but if you'll just give us an appointment, I'll get him in here somehow.

Th: Let me say something because I think it could save a lot of time if I could have a chance—at least in that first session— just to sit down with you, Mrs. Cooper, because if your husband has had a bad experience, and he was not giving it his best try that time, that could happen again. And getting together with you, at least first, might give me a clearer idea as to how to help him with his motivation on it. So, mainly, could we set up an appointment so I could just have a chance to sit down with you that first time at least?

Pt: Then you wouldn't want to see my husband at all?

Th: Not the first time. Now, if you . . . I'd like you to mention to him that you've set up the appointment, and that I haven't explained why—at least fully—but that I just wanted to see you. If he insists on coming in, that's OK. But if he maintains the reluctance that I gather you're indicating, then you just come on in by yourself.

Pt: OK, I guess that would be all right.

Th: All right. And how about if we set it up for this coming Tuesday at 2:00?

Pt: Yeah, that should be fine.

Th: Fine. I'll look forward to meeting you then.

In this second example, a male patient calls to make an appointment for treatment and while on the phone attempts to describe his problem and negotiate a prescription for medicine:

Th: Hello.

Pt: Hello, is this Dr. French?

Th: Yes, speaking.

Pt: I'm calling you to see if I can arrange an appointment to see you. I've just moved here from Chicago, and I've been in therapy there for awhile—oh, about two years. I've been seeing Dr. James; do you know him?

Th: No, I'm afraid I don't.

Pt: Well, he said that I should look you up when I got here— I don't know where he got your name—and said that he would be in contact with you to let you know what he has been doing with me. Have you gotten his letter yet?

Th: No, I haven't received anything from him. And your name is what, sir?

Pt: Oh, my name is Joe.

Th: Joe?

Pt: Joe Smith.

Th: OK, Mr. Smith. No, I haven't gotten anything from him.

Pt: Oh, well, then he probably hasn't gotten around to writing it yet. I thought it would be there by this time. Anyhow, I've been having this problem for a couple of years, and, like I say, I've been in therapy with him. And I was wondering if I could come in and see you about it.

Th: So I gather you're calling to set up an appointment, then?

Pt: Yes, I think that would probably be the best idea. This problem has been bugging me for a long time, and I'd like to . . . maybe I could tell you some more about it so that we could do something before we arrange the appointment.

Th: Well, let me interrupt. I'm one of those people who have difficulty digesting any important information over a phone, so that if whatever it is you need to say is important—and I assume it is—I really can do it better justice if we can sit down face to face. So I think it would be much better to save that until we can get together.

Pt: OK. Then I guess I would like to see if I could get an appointment with you as soon as possible.

Th: OK. What's your schedule like as far as mornings or afternoons go?

Pt: Well, I work in the mornings and afternoons and would really like to come in in the evening.

Th: Unfortunately, the latest I would be seeing people is at 4:00 in the afternoon. I start at 8:00 and by 5:00 I've reached my human limit, and I'm not much good to anybody after that.

Pt: Then is there any chance that I could see you on the weekend?

Th: Well, I usually recommend that my patients enjoy their weekends, and I don't want to be a hypocrite; so, unless there's an emergency, I don't set up appointments on the weekends. I'm afraid we would be limited to sometime Monday through Friday, either at 8:00 somewhere or no later than 4:00. If you're working, it might be less inconvenient if it were one end of the day or the other. Is that right?

Pt: Yes, yes.

Th: Let me just check my schedule, then.

Pt: OK.

Th: I could make it either 8:00 on Tuesday morning or 4:00 on Thursday afternoon, whichever would be less inconvenient for you.

Pt: 8:00 on Monday?

Th: 8:00 on Tuesday or 4:00 on Thursday.

Pt: OK, and then I'd be able to start next week?

Th: Yes, we could get together. This is next week, right?

Pt: And should I then phone Dr. James and see if he has gotten the records to you?

Th: You can do that, but my preference is to get things straight first from the person I'm going to be working with, and then after that to get any other people's impressions, like previous therapists. So I'd rather get it straight from you first because this involves you and your problem. And then after that it would probably be valuable to get your previous therapist's views too.

Pt: OK. I guess that's the way I have to do it, then.

Th: OK. I think you have my address, so without going into . . . Oh, I just forgot—which day would you prefer, the Tuesday at 8:00 or the Thursday at 4:00?

Pt: Well, what I'd really prefer would be the Tuesday at 8:00.

Th: All right, let's set it up for then, and let's meet then at that time, and I'll look forward to meeting you and we can get on with things.

Pt: I assume that in seeing you I can probably get a refill on the prescription for the medication I've been getting before?

Th: I don't know. I think I'd have to sit down with you first and get some idea, at least, of the problem and whether it would be useful to have the medication or not. I really just don't know about that right now.

Pt: OK. We'll keep it that way, then, and I'll see you on Tuesday.

❧ 4 ❧

The Initial
Interview

The therapist's main aim in the initial interview is to gather adequate information on the elements we see as basic to every case: the nature of the complaint, how the problem is being handled, the client's minimal goals, and the client's position and language. By "adequate" we mean information that is clear, explicit, and in behavioral terms —what specific individuals say and do in *performing* the problem and in their attempts to deal with it, rather than general statements or explanatory interpretations such as "We don't communicate," "Johnny has a school phobia," or "I lack self-confidence because my mother neglected me." Adequate information is a prerequisite for brief but effective treatment, since it constitutes the foundation on which interventions are planned and carried out. To get such information may require considerable time, effort, and persistence, but this will be well spent. It is much better to make haste slowly at the start than to press on toward some sort of active intervention—"doing something"—before the problem and its handling have been made clear and explicit.

How is such information to be obtained? Ordinarily, one should begin simply by asking, "What is the problem that brings you to see me?" By this we mean the problem *now*. We do not attach much importance to the history of problems, although it is useful to have some information on how long a problem has existed and whether there has been prior treatment—mainly because these may influence patient expectations about the present therapy. Therefore, if a client seems to be getting involved in a long historical account, we will indicate that our main concern is with the current status of the problem: "Somehow I can understand better by hearing first where things are at now, and then working backward in time, rather than the other way around." Most patients will accept this, since the therapist is not downgrading the importance of past history. A few patients, however, insist on delving into the past. Then the better alternative is for the therapist to listen patiently, and wait until later to obtain a clear statement of the problem at present, rather than get into an argument about it.

In addition to this focus on what is present or current, our inquiry focuses on the chief *complaint* or complaints of those seeking help, in behavioral terms: "*Who* is doing *what* that presents a problem, to *whom,* and *how* does such behavior constitute a problem?" Of course, the therapist will not ask this complex question all at once; but direct inquiry, part by part, is usually the best way to begin. In the following example, a mother has brought her daughter, the identified patient, to an initial interview:

Th: Why don't we just start out, and can you describe to me what the problem is that brings you in today? I want to hear from both of you, so whichever wants to start . . .

M: It's a long story. I don't know, it just seems to me that it has been going on forever, really. Looking back, I just don't—I've never—nobody ever told me what's wrong with Barbara. I know she is not improving. She feels safe in the state hospital where she is taken care of.

Th: How long has she been up there?

D: Was it June or July? I forget now . . .

M: Yes, that's her second time up there, within the last twelve months, I guess. It's always short term—four months or so. Two months. But then she feels . . . very good, and then she feels she's ready to go out and . . . She can take normal outside living —well, we found out, about three weeks—and then she starts on a down cycle. She gets very depressed and, using her words for it, she says, "Mom, I get paranoid. First I have the feeling people are staring, and then I feel people are going to attack me, and then I have to do something about that." And what she does then is, she'll either pick up a knife or a piece of glass and cut herself.

Th: Cuts herself?

M: Yes, very badly. She—her arms are cut up. Or she will attack another person, which unfortunately . . . She has had about three incidents where the police had to step in.

Th: Has she seriously hurt anyone else in these attacks?

M: Well, not seriously yet, but close enough to draw blood, and this is one worry I have every time. When she's not in the hospital, every time the phone is ringing, I am in fear, you know? What now?

Th: Whom did she attack?

M: She has attacked counselors. She has attacked her sister. She has never directly attacked me. She sat in front of me with a screwdriver in one hand and a knife in the other. But she did not attack me. She did attack her sister. And that's when I felt it was just too dangerous to have her living . . .

Th: But mostly she does this to herself?

M: Mostly she does it to herself.

If an answer is not clear and specific, the therapist should not act as if it is, but rather say, "I'm not clear on that," taking the overt onus on himself (instead of saying, "You're too vague"), and ask for a restatement. Such questioning often must be persistent and firm, though polite. Requesting an example of the problem often is the best way to get specific and concrete behavioral information. More than one *who* may be involved in a problem (for instance, two difficult children in one family), there may be different forms of the *what* (for example, various bizarre actions by a schizophrenic), and the behavior may constitute a problem for more than one person (for both parents of a difficult child or for the whole staff involved with an institutionalized patient). But such multiplicity should be summarizable into simple classes of behaviors and persons. Unless the therapist can make a brief and clear statement covering all the elements in the presenting complaint (*who, what, to whom,* and *how*), he either does not have adequate information on the complaint or he has not digested the information sufficiently, and to proceed further without clearly formulating the problem will lead to trouble. Essentially, he will be working without a clear picture; and as additional and varied information is accumulated through further interviews, it will not be easier but harder to formulate the problem concisely.

Even those therapists who plainly ask, "What is the problem?" may fail to ask, "*How* is the situation you mention a problem?" Sometimes, it is true, *how* a situation is a problem is plain. But in any case of uncertainty, it is better for a therapist to appear dull and slow than to feign understanding when matters are not really clear. For instance, a young married couple came in about the wife's "drinking problem," although she was at most drinking a fifth of table wine in a day:

Th: You were starting to say before that the level of drinking you're doing is affecting your life.

Pt: Uh-huh.

Th: And also your health. Could you fill me in as to how it's affecting you in those ways?

Pt: Well, the doctor told me a year ago that I had fat in my liver, and I—sometimes after a night when I've been drinking heavily, I can feel it back here, and I know that I do again, and I . . .

Th: Have you had any reexamination, or . . .

Pt: No, and I was supposed to go and I haven't gone back.

And I haven't had regular periods for two years, and as a matter of fact I haven't had one for about four or five months now. For a while the doctor put me on folic acid, and that seemed to bring them back. And then that ran out because I haven't been back to see him; I haven't been taking it again. I've gained about fifteen to twenty pounds, which was very depressing, obviously. So those are health things, you know. I mean, I just—my body's just not functioning quite right. As far as my life goes, it doesn't really bother my work too much because, I mean, not really much at all because I only work two days a week, and I have lots of time to . . . I mean, that's not really been a problem. But, um, you know, I know it bothers my husband a lot, and it's not real great for our sex life since I tend to be half in the bag when it's time to go to bed, many times. Um, I think I'm more . . . When I don't feel good—or feel bad about myself, because I gave in to drinking the night before, or whatever—I think I tend to be a lot harsher on the children, a lot quicker. You know, just . . . when one doesn't feel very good about oneself, one doesn't treat others as well as they should be; sometimes I'm too hard on them, I think.

Th: Well, OK. In any other way does it interfere with your life or affect your life?

Pt: Um . . .

Th: Socially, or . . .

Pt: Well, it hasn't happened in a while. It seems things have been fairly good for a while, but there have been times—as a matter of fact, I guess, before we first went to see [a previous therapist], and then after that sometimes, that we would go— we would be either at a party or out to dinner, and I would get noticeably—when I drink I become very disoriented, motorically—I don't know if that's a word!—my motor skills become way off. And it's very embarrassing to my husband, and . . .

Th: What do you do?

Pt: Well, I have a hard time walking.

Th: Do you fall down?

Pt: Sometimes. I have a hard time, you know, eating without spilling something on myself, you know. That kind of thing. And . . .

Th: And it's embarrassing to . . .

H: It's embarrassing to me.

Th: . . . to your husband, so I was just wondering if it's embarrassing to your friends, or do they find it amusing?

Pt: Um . . .

Th: Because that kind of thing can be funny, you know.

Pt: I think it's been funny on occasion, but I think that generally it's a little bit embarrassing. And I think that, although I've never discussed even going to a counselor or anything, with anyone—except my husband and my own parents—I think they realize that that is a problem with me.

From this interview—although further inquiry is needed to check the matter out—it begins to appear as if the drinking may embarrass and upset the husband more than it interferes with the wife's own daily life.

There are at least three (somewhat overlapping) common situations where this "How" inquiry may be critical. First are those cases where a reported "problem" seems to be a minor matter. Careful inquiry is then essential to determine whether in some way the behavior is more serious than first appeared; or whether the client is overconcerned about something but can be directly reassured, which is rather rare; or whether the client is seriously "making a mountain out of a molehill." This last constitutes a serious problem in itself, though a different one than seriously deviant overt behavior, and one that facile reassurance will only exacerbate. Second, clients may present as "problems" difficulties that, even if severe, other people recognize as vicissitudes of life that cannot be changed and simply must be lived with. To recognize this at least helps the therapist avoid enmeshment in attempts to change the unchangeable. Finally, some problems of life are not a therapist's province but call, for example, for the help of a lawyer, a physician, or a financial counselor. The "How is it a problem?" question helps clarify this point and may need to be followed up by "How do you see me as being helpful in dealing with that problem?"

In addition to "What is the problem?" a subsidiary question often needs to be asked: "How did you come to call me at the particular time you did, rather than sooner or later?" Information gained about the circumstances precipitating or surrounding this initial action often throws new light on what the problem is. For example, it can reveal that the client is not herself much concerned about the stated problem but that someone else has put her under duress:

Th: How did you come to seek treatment at this particular time?

Pt: My father suggested it to me. My car is in the shop, and I was talking to him because it had been in there for three weeks and it was only supposed to take three days. And I was asking him whether there was something I could do about it or whether I was getting too upset. And I guess he thought I was getting too upset.

Th: OK, so he suggested it, and your mother called. It sort of leaves me wondering . . .

Pt: I think she called beforehand, and then she talked to him about it.

Th: Uh-huh.

Pt: And then he suggested it. See, they sometimes have these little discussions that you don't know about.

Th: If they weren't suggesting, would you be here?

Pt: No. I was thinking of seeking something on my own.

Th: What might that have been?

Pt: It's something that my mother told me about a while ago, in San Francisco. A person for . . . I mean, a place for child abuse, where I could go for free. And my mother told me about it after—when I was a senior, when a special counselor at school tried to seduce me. And so I ended up telling somebody about it, and she left the school. And there's been a couple other things like that that have happened to me. And I kind of thought it would be nice to get those straightened out. Thought it could fit in pretty well with the way that I relate to people. So I'm kind of suspicious, I guess, of people.

Th: Uh-huh. You have reason to be. They aren't all out there looking out for you.

Pt: I know.

Th: Well, I don't know, we're in sort of a, perhaps, slightly funny position here, since what we've just been talking about . . . You've sort of been sent rather than being here under your own steam.

Pt: Yeah, like I feel that now because I'm sitting here feeling like I don't really need it that badly.

Th: Well, you may very well be right. And it could be, in a sense, something worse than that. What I'm thinking about is, while I'm by no means sure—I haven't gotten enough information for any sweeping conclusions—some of the things you've been saying have at least a little ring of—perhaps with the best intentions, your family's a little bit on your back about what you ought to be doing and how you ought to be performing, and here you are here, also under their aegis, and I'm not sure that's a whale of a starting place.

Pt: Yeah, I sort of feel like I have my father hanging over me, back here, saying, "Yes, you're supposed to get here and get all straightened out so you can start performing up to par as well as your sister," or something.

Similar situations occur when an offender has been sent to treatment by an agent of the law, or one spouse has been sent by the other. The handling of such cases differs from that for the self-motivated, as discussed in Chapter Two.

The next step is to ask what all the persons closely involved with the problem have been doing to try to handle or resolve it. Those closely involved, in addition to the patient, may include family members, friends, fellow workers, professionals, and so on, according to the circumstances of the particular case. Again, this inquiry focuses on actual behaviors—what are people *doing* and *saying* in their attempts to prevent a recurrence of the problem, or to deal with it when it does happen?

Th: When your daughter starts appearing depressed and letting her appearance go and so forth, what do you do at that time to try to change things around?

M: Well, as long as she was home, I tried to either be cheerful or try to talk to her, which is impossible. When it comes to this point, you cannot talk to her.

Th: What happens? What does . . .

M: She . . . It has always been that when I try to talk to her she would turn away from me, just like this. And, you know, "Just go ahead and talk. I don't care what you say." And this has gone on till she was in the hospital the first time. Then I saw a change in her; then all of a sudden she started listening to me, she would talk to me. She would, more or less, open up to you. She would say things to me which she had never done before; she would say, "I love you, Mommy. I need you."

Th: Is this when she first got out of the state hospital, then?

M: Yes. Before that, there was no way. She would turn her back, and I was talking against a blank wall. But since the hospital, she . . .

Th: I'm still a little unclear. When she starts to say—you know, she acts as if she's feeling depressed, and says things like "People are staring at me" and this type of thing—specifically, what do you say to her? Do you . . .

M: Well, that is—she just starting telling me that. I would say two months ago was the first time. And that was when she was at the county hospital, after she had . . .

Th: All right, but how did you respond to that, when she said that?

M: I remember I put my arms around her, and I tried to, you know, be gentle with her, be loving. I don't know what else I . . .

Th: And what did you say?

M: I told her that I understood, that that could be very true, because I think you can get that feeling when people, you know, with people, I don't know. Sometimes it's difficult for me to understand. Sometimes I had the feeling when she was at the county hospital, before she went to the state hospital two months ago, that I just wanted to shake her, you know? And just say, "Snap out of it!" But then I know she can't. I mean . . .

Th: So you didn't do that?

M: No. I didn't. I just—I knew she wanted me there, which was more than we have ever had before. So I just more or less stayed with her, held her hand, put my arm around her.

Th: OK. Earlier, when you said that you would try to talk with her, when you noticed her sliding downhill like that. What sort of talk? Were you just trying to hold light conversation, or were you commenting on what she was doing, or . . .

M: Well, when she was small enough to sit on my lap, I would ask her to come sit on Mommy's lap, and let's just, you know, be quiet a little bit, and she would always fight me.

Th: How about more recently? Since she's been bigger?

M: I can really only see the difference last—really the last six months—because before that I felt resentment.

Th: She would turn her back on you.

M: She just resented me, and she wouldn't listen, she turned her back. And I know that . . .

Th: What did you do when she turned her back? Did you walk around her? Did you grab her shoulder? Did you say, "Listen to me"?

M: I tried that, and it didn't work. I don't know. Finally, I was so . . . I got discouraged and depressed, and I just didn't know how to handle it anymore.

Th: So what did you do?

M: Well, when she was younger, I used to get angry. And then I said to myself: "Well, that's not really the way to handle it. To yell at her." She could do that to me; she could make me really yell at her. And then I felt guilty that I lost my temper, that I even spanked her. Because I think I tried to bring her up the way I was brought up, which was very strict European upbringing.

As with inquiries about the problem itself, some clients will give clear and direct answers fairly readily, but others will be vague, general, or tangential or will offer interpretations rather than descriptions of behavior. Persistent inquiry will be necessary in such cases. Since such persistence can convey badgering the client, or imply that the client is inept in making himself understood, the therapist can avoid these implications by prefacing his continuing inquiry with an explanation that puts the onus on himself for "not understanding": "Please bear with me. I have a very concrete mind, so could you give me an example or two of what you've tried?"

Inquiry about clients' minimal goals of treatment is likely to prove more difficult than inquiries about the problem and its handling. It is best to be aware of this probability, and not to interpret any difficulty in getting a clear and specific answer as a sign of resistance or pathology. Uncertain, vague, or sweeping answers are common, since patients are like all of us: we are clearer about what we don't want than about what we do want. Despite such probable difficulties, it is important to raise this question and to pursue it: "What, if it were to happen, would you see as a first sign that a significant—though maybe small— change had occurred?" In a fair proportion of cases, some pertinent answer will be obtained with reasonable effort. Even if not, the question serves a significant function in conveying that the therapist is concerned with and aiming toward observable behavioral change, of a small but significant sort.

As mentioned earlier, many clients present difficulties even in this early information-gathering stage of treatment. We cannot cover all the possible difficulties here. Therapy is always a matter of dealing effectively with what each particular client presents, and this can never be completely predicted and prepared for in advance. Nevertheless, we can identify and discuss a few such difficulties.

We may center this discussion around responses to the

simplest question, "What is the problem?" since this comes first
and difficulties with the other questions, and the means of handling them, are likely to be similar in nature. First, many clients
—especially those who are psychologically sophisticated and
those with previous experience of therapy—often give a causal
or dynamic formulation *about* the problem instead of specify-
ing the behavior constituting it. Such formulations may be specific or, as in the following example, very general:

Pt: OK, OK. I think 90 percent of the problem is figuring out
what the problem is. So, you know, I can't just kind of lay it on
you, like, you know, I'm wetting my bed or something like
that. So I'm just gonna start talking about it. Um, I think, I
think that I—I sense that I'm at a certain kind of stage in my
life where—which is a very important stage in my life, you
know. It's kind of a—it's a watershed of some sort; I'm making
some kind of transition into the next stage and it's . . . I'm learning things about myself or about the person that I'm becoming,
and a lot of the things which had been real to me, and values
kind of which had guided me in the past are falling away, or are
no longer giving me the kind of support I need. So that right
now, in my life, as I see my life, and I see the kind of task before me, there's a lot of—there's a lot of obstacles which I'm up
against, which I have to kind of figure out—figure out how to
deal with them.

Th: Can you give me an example of any of those obstacles?

Pt: No, I mean . . . I mean . . . For me, everything is connected, OK? Everything in my life relates to everything else in
my life, so it's—so I can't, you know, I mean . . .

Th: OK, but can you just give me an example of one?

Pt: Sure. Sure.

Th: What would be an obstacle?

Pt: There's two. All right, there's two kinds of areas in which
I kind of feel are key problems. And they're my work and my
sex life. But everything . . . I mean, they are related to each
other, and it relates to my diet, and it relates to my, you know
. . . Every aspect of my life-style is tied up with that.

Th: Give me an example of how your work would be an obstacle; how is it an obstacle to you?

Pt: Work isn't an obstacle. Work is, you know, a theme, and what I'm trying to do is figure out . . .

Th: Well, you said everything is an obstacle, and I'm just trying to . . .

Pt: No, I didn't mean to say everything is an obstacle; everything is a—is a theme in which obstacles inhere.

A therapist usually can handle this kind of difficulty by stating that, before going on to the deeper level of causation, he needs to get a clear view of how the problem is manifested. He can also persistently ask for examples and specifics: "Imagine that I am photographing a scene representative of the problem. What picture and dialogue would the camera be picking up?" On a few occasions, we have asked people to bring in an outline of a skit illustrating the problem, in which the therapists will play the roles of the family members while the client will act as director, cuing the "actors" on their lines, movements, and tonality. While seemingly time consuming, this procedure can actually save time with clients whose verbal descriptions are unclear.

Other clients, instead of offering causal explanations, may begin by stating one problem, but then shift in midstream to another, then a third, and so on. Once this shifting about becomes evident, the therapist must take action to get some single focus defined (or, in sessions with a couple or a family, at least one focus for each person). If not, he is likely to find himself in fruitless pursuit of a client, moving from one thing to another as long as the therapy goes on. The simplest way to deal with this problem, and probably the best in most cases, is for the therapist to ask the client to define his priorities. This can best be done from a one-down position: "I can see that a lot of problems are on your mind, but my capacity to grasp things—let alone deal with them—is too limited to grapple with a lot of things all at once. I just get muddled. So would you tell me what strikes you as the main problem right now, the one that is most important to change, if possible?" When such a choice is

made, the client can legitimately be reminded of it if he begins
to shift again: "You said initially that X was the most important problem to work on, but now you seem to be focusing on
Y. Of course, we could focus on Y if that now seems more important. We'd only have to start all over again." As this example suggests, when difficulties arise, even the ordinarily simple
matter of information gathering may require strategic handling
rather than direct inquiry. More persistent shifting about,
though less common if the above measures are taken, might require stronger strategic moves. For example, the therapist might
suggest that the topic shifted away from, though it is the most
important, is probably just too difficult or painful to talk
about. Or the therapist might even shift the focus before the
client does, so that the client now must try to keep the therapist on the main track.

Grandiose responses occur most often in replies to goal
inquiries—it is staggering what some people propose as a "minimal" step—but may even appear in stating the problem: "Everything is wrong," "I'm a total mess," or, California style, "I
haven't achieved full self-actualization." Persistent requests for
information on how the problem affects daily life, and for specific examples, usually help. In very difficult cases, it may be
necessary and useful to go to a greater extreme, to outdo the
client along similar lines, to suggest he is thinking too small—so
that, again, he finds it important to get the therapist down to
business.

Certain clients may disrupt the whole process of information gathering. Active disrupters include schizophrenics who
"talk crazy" and noisy or otherwise disturbing children. Passive
disrupters may indicate that they are too uncertain or too overcome by emotions to answer much, or at the extreme act mute.
Where possible, the best way to handle all these situations is to
get rid of the uncommunicative individual, who is seldom the
chief complainant anyway, and work with family members or
others who are seriously concerned about the problem. (This
important matter of whom the therapist should choose to see is
discussed in Chapter Three.) If the therapist must work with an
uncommunicative client, he should state simply and plainly that

he needs certain information in order to be of any possible help and that he is dependent on the client for this information. Then he should sit back. Active encouragement or pressing the client to talk should be avoided. It may even be useful for the therapist to state that the client perhaps should not speak out, and to give reasons why this might be so.

In the following example, the patient is a young man in his early twenties; it is his second session:

Th: You'll have to excuse me today as I am recovering from the flu, as you probably pick up by my congested voice; I may be a bit slow. OK, I went over the tape of the last session, and there were some questions that I wanted to ask you about that. I was a little unclear last week. I was a little unclear about exactly what the problem is that you have come in to see us about.

Pt: [Long pause] Well, I think I'm very unclear on it too.

Th: OK.

Pt: [Long pause] Well, someone to ask questions. I need someone to ask questions.

Th: Oh, OK.

Pt: Ones that I can't ask myself or haven't thought of. A sounding board, as I said. Of course, that isn't the problem, though, is it?

Th: [Pause] Well, I could ask you some questions; I mean, I could ask you standard kinds of questions. Where would you see that going, though? What would be the goal of that, what would you get out of it?

Pt: [Long pause] Well... [Long pause] Some insight into what I'm doing. Maybe why I'm doing it. [Pause] Yeah. Insight into what I'm doing, and if I have any reasons behind it.

Th: OK. Could you give me some idea about what it is you're doing, then, that you'd like to have insight into? What would you like to change, maybe?

Pt: [Long pause] I really don't know.

Th: There's just one thing I wanted to bring up; it's been an issue for this session and the last session. It's that I've noticed that there are periods of silence when I ask you a question sometimes. And I know it's your right to be like that, and I just wanted you to know that I feel somewhat uncomfortable with that silence.

Pt: Mmm, I'm trying to think.

Th: You can think aloud if you wish.

Pt: I'll try. I just draw blanks sometimes once the question is asked. I have to think back to what I've been doing, what I haven't been doing.

Th: Uh-huh. Well, my colleagues who are observing called me in because they pointed out that I was getting off track, in terms of finding out from you and asking you what is your problem—what is the problem that you came in here about. That, to some extent, I've gotten off track with the dramatic talk about suicide in the first session. But that we do have a time-limited framework within which to work—ten sessions—and that I should get back and ask you what's the problem that you came in about, that you took the trouble to make the call to come out here. What are the troubles you've having? [Pause] Because we really can't proceed without that information. [Long pause]

Pt: What are the problems I'm having? [Long pause] I draw a blank. [Pause] General incompetence in handling my life. [Pause] What *are* the problems I'm having?

Th: Could you give me a specific example of your incompetence in handling your life?

Pt: [Pause] Well, the house is a mess, I'm broke, and all I feel like doing is laying in bed all day.

Th: How is that a problem? I mean, some people take time out and just hang out.

Pt: Uh-huh. [Long pause] I don't know. [Pause] I just ... I'm drawing a blank. [JW enters.]

JW: I don't know about [the primary therapist], but some of the rest of us are also sort of concrete-minded. I am. We really felt, OK, we heard you when you said you're broke, your house is a mess, and you're just sort of lying around all day.

Pt: Uh-huh.

JW: That's the beginning of saying something about a problem that at least we can get through our heads, so we thought we ought to let you know that. Of course, people always get asked for more when they do something good, so you know where it's gonna go from there.

Pt: All right. Concretes. The house is a mess, I'm broke, I'm lying in bed. [Pause]

Th: Well, how long have you been doing that?

Pt: OK, yeah. Well, since the end of the summer. I started back to school in the end of September, and that sort of broke it up for a couple weeks. Then my schedule was just impossible. I had to work the night before and then be in class until 4:30, so I decided—I didn't even decide—I just ... One day I just didn't make it, and then—figuring I could make it up—and then later the next day. Not even the next one, I guess. A week later, and microbiology labs—you just can't miss them like that. And I got sort of caught up and overwhelmed. So I haven't even dropped out officially yet. Uh, I have rather my doubts that I can. At this point. Yeah, that's got me down, I guess. It's ...

Th: These are difficulties to do with your schoolwork.

Pt: Uh-huh. Yeah.

Th: Well, what was the problem with that now? You were enrolled in school ...

Pt: Uh-huh.

Th: In fact, you still are.

Pt: Yes.

Th: Have you been going to classes, then?

Pt: No. No, that was it. I've dropped them, but I haven't officially dropped them. Uhh, it's making a decision without making a decision. Uhh ...

Th: And so, if I'm clear, you . . . What you've done with the
school stuff is just to kind of make a decision without making a
decision—just not turning up.

Pt: Uh-huh.

Th: Have you been in touch with any of your professors?

Pt: No. [Pause] I didn't enroll this semester until the first day
of classes. I didn't really want to go back to school. Why did I?
Oh, because my mother kept bugging me, and—I do want to go
back to school.

Finally, and perhaps most difficult, are clients who talk
readily enough but are persistently vague:

Th: What is the problem that brings you in today?

Pt: Basically, I was—I read about your program in the newspaper or a publication of the University of California—I don't
remember where. What attracted me to you was the fact that I
was interested in seeing somebody, but I wanted to confine the
exploration to a certain area. You know? So instead of getting
into an extended program, and my wife had been—had seen psy-
chiatrists in the past. And the impression I got was that the situation went on and on and on without really reaching a goal or
without really getting any feeling—OK, I'm making progress or
not—it was rather nebulous. Back East, before we came here to
California, eleven years ago, I had seen somebody for a short
period of time—a Jungian. And I had the impression that in
some cases I was just treading water. Now, that is a sort of introduction—what brought me here. What is the specific problem
I have in mind? Uh, basically, I would like to get a better understanding about my personal goals, in terms of . . . Can I have
something clearly established in my own mind to look at my
life and decide: "Yes, I have really accomplished something" or
"I have been just floating from one place to the other, and sort
of fighting battles, and trying to do things without any sense of
a real direction, or a goal, or an objective." I have to say that
many times I have been torn between my obligations to myself,
my obligations to my wife, my obligations to my children, my

obligations to my family here, my obligations to my original family, who is in South America. And sometimes I get very, very angry with myself in the sense that I have been getting . . . I get the impression that in the past I have put too many people ahead of me in terms of the allocation of time, allocation of resources . . . And sometimes I have been kind of too, too nice—to try to compromise and try to just go along, as opposed to saying, "OK, this is what I would like to do." Today you find me at the rather interesting point in the sense that I am in the process of changing jobs, sort of redirecting my career. And I consider that the coming fifteen years—ten or fifteen years—will be of tremendous importance in my life. And I would like to get to a point where I can really feel that I have explored with some . . . What are the things, what are my goals? What are my different roles? What is the priority? How can I more or less compromise or optimize the situation? And the other point is that I'm not . . . I realize that if somebody were to look at me and explore what I have done in the past, a person could point out many, many areas where I need work. I realize that. My feeling is that I am not that much interested in the situation of *maximizing* but just getting to the point of *optimizing*. And that is an area where my wife and I have had some differences of opinion. My feeling is that in looking at . . . My feeling is that there are many people who can get along fine. Some other people need some help. Now, there are some other people who have to be . . .

Th: Let's just take that situation and see what we can learn from that. You say you feel there are things to be done for work.

Pt: Well, I have to explain. Probably a sort of introduction might be appropriate. I was born in South America. I came to the States in 1959. I went to school here, in accounting. I got married at a rather late age, by usual standards; when I got married, I was thirty-eight, and my wife was thirty. From that point of view, in the years I have been here, when I count on the fact that I grew up in an entirely different environment, it has been necessary for me to do a tremendous amount of catching up.

Catching up, more or less becoming, sort of changing my way of thinking. I grew up—I was educated in a very, very strict environment, where there were formal rules in sort of a very, very strict . . .

If no headway is made by the usual requests ("I'm not clear on that. I have a concrete sort of mind. Could you bear with me and give me an example of what you are talking about?"), it is useless and worse to keep on this fruitless course: "Always change a losing game." One possible strategic tack, though its application to this situation is relatively little tested and needs further exploration, is to best the client at his own game, ultimately for his own benefit. For instance, the therapist might display even more confusion and vagueness than the client, or alternatively say, "Aha! Now I've got what the problem is!" and confidently state something which, in his best guess, is certainly *not* what the client is talking around. At the ultimate, the only way to deal with this problem—which we see as posing great obstacles to all forms of psychotherapy, not just our own—may be to ignore the obscure subject matter and move to a higher level; that is, to take the vagueness as itself the most significant problem and seek ways to change it.

In the first interview, it is also important to get at least some initial grasp of the client's language or position; but this type of information, discussed in the following chapter, is of a different order and is not gained mainly by direct inquiry.

❧ 5 ❧

Patient
Position

The therapist can know what he would like the patient to do to resolve his problem, but gaining his cooperation in the doing of it is another matter—especially since, as we have emphasized, the patient's problem-engendering "solution" is determined by what he regards as the only reasonable, sane, or life-saving thing to do, despite its failure to resolve his problem. Therefore, getting the patient to let go of his own "solution" and, instead, to undertake an approach he would ordinarily consider crazy or dangerous is a vital step in doing therapy briefly. It is in this task that patient position plays a critical role. In this chapter, we will be expanding on that aspect of information and its use, describing what we mean by "position," what its importance in treatment is, how "position" can be assessed, and, finally, how "patient position" can be used to increase the cooperation of the patient and, therefore, the success of treatment.

In essence, the principal task of therapy is to influence the client to deal differently with his problem or complaint. But *how* we influence another in large part depends on *whom* we are attempting to influence. It is not simply that there are different suggestions one might make; it is, even more, how *any* suggestion is framed. *How* we put something may be persuasive to one person but not to another. For example, both the bon vivant and the economy-minded person may buy a Rolls Royce, but for obviously different reasons—the bon vivant because of the distinctiveness and status of the car; the other because the engineering and durability of the car can save him money in the long run. Because of these differences in appeal, the salesman needs to make his sales talk different for each customer. How he frames his sales talk can make the difference between customer acceptance or rejection.

Patients are people too, and have their own strongly held beliefs, values, and priorities, which determine how they will act or not act. Thus, the importance of "position" is that it represents an inclination within patients which can be utilized to enhance the acceptance and carrying out of therapist directives. When the Rolls Royce salesman confronted by the economy-minded customer emphasizes the engineering and durability of the car, he is enlisting the values ("position") of the customer toward buying it. If, instead, he extolled its virtue as a status symbol, he would fail to tap the customer's own momentum and would actively drive him away; he would not be talking the customer's "language."

There are many terms or phrases we could have used to refer to patients' beliefs, but we have chosen "position" because it is a succinct way of indicating a value to which a client is committed and has gone on record about, much as a public figure makes a "position statement." Knowing what the client's position is allows one to formulate guidelines on how to couch —or frame—a suggestion in a way that the client is most likely to accept. We believe that persuasion has always played a significant role in psychotherapy, as it does in all other aspects of human interaction. Instead of claiming that persuasion does not or should not exist in the treatment context, we believe it is inescapable and therefore deserving of explicit recognition and of more disciplined use. In this chapter, we are talking about a more efficient "persuasion," one that *uses* the patient's position to facilitate cooperation and thus aid in the resolution of his problem.

Assessing Patient Position

Assuming, then, that the therapist is interested in using this kind of leverage, how can he assess the positions his patient is taking, which might be used to expedite treatment most effectively? To begin with, as in all data gathering, it is important to listen to what the patient *says*: What specific wording does he use, and with what tone and emphases does he express himself? Two very different positions can be expressed by similar wording: In response to a therapist's comment, a patient can say either "Yes. [Pause] I see how that fits" or "Yes, I can see how that's *possible*." In the first statement, the patient is indicating "I agree with you and have accepted your comment." In the second statement, he is implying "I don't agree with you but prefer not to make that explicit at this time." At least, some doubt or reservation is implicit. If the therapist is not listening to the precise phrasing and intonation, he is likely to accept the second statement as agreement, and then be puzzled when the patient subsequently fails to *implement* his suggestion.

People can have definite and strongly held views on everything under the sun and beyond. (Practically speaking, even firm indifference on an issue is a position. As Sam Goldwyn allegedly replied to a proposed deal, "I can give you a definite maybe on that.") It is impossible for a patient to express all his views, but fortunately it is not necessary for the therapist to know all of them. For purposes of treatment, the therapist will need to be attentive to the patient's position in regard to his complaint and in regard to treatment and/or the therapist. While patients may convey positions on other facets of their lives—for example, whether they view themselves as unique or as part of the mainstream—and while these other kinds of posi-

tions can also be used to expedite cooperation, these two principal areas will be most important in formulating plans for enhancing patient cooperation. The two areas will often overlap,
but we will discuss them separately for greater clarity.

Generally, coming to a therapist is in itself an acknowledgment by the patient that he is troubled by his problem, that he
has been unsuccessful in handling it on his own, and that he is
now seeking help from the therapist. Nevertheless, many—if not
most—patients will still have notions regarding the nature of
their problem and its presumed cause, as well as some general or
specific ideas about how it can be resolved. Often they will express these notions in the course of describing the problem and
its history. If the therapist ignores these "position statements,"
he can blunder into a strategy that will be met with resistance;
this at best will consume considerable nonproductive time and
may well alienate the client. For example, two sets of parents
may have basically the same complaint, some form of troublesome behavior by their teenage child. Yet each set of parents
can state the complaint in very different terms and thereby express very different positions—positions that will require different "sales talks" by the therapist:

> Set A: "We have come in because of *concern*
> about our fifteen-year-old son. He has been having ex-
> treme *difficulty adjusting* to the *demands* of school.
> We believe his *underlying unhappiness* is being *ex-
> pressed* in *aggressiveness* to other boys in our neigh-
> borhood, and sometimes to us. We are *fearful* that he
> may be headed for a more serious *breakdown.*"
>
> Set B: "We have come in because of total *frus-
> tration* in *controlling* our fifteen-year-old son. He
> *won't* do a *lick of work* at school, even when he *de-
> cides* to attend, and now he is *picking fights* with
> other kids in our neighborhood. He has gotten so
> *nasty* at home that we decided *we needed* some *help.*"

As the italicized words and expressions indicate, the parents in Set A have a sympathetic point of view. In essence, they
regard their son's misbehavior as "sick." In contrast, the parents
in Set B are angry. They regard their son as willful, as uncaring

about others, and, essentially, as "bad." While the goals of treatment are likely to be much the same—improvement in the boys'
school performances and relationships in the neighborhood and
at home—and the recommended specific actions may be similar
in both cases, the strategies and the framing of the recommended
actions will be quite different. For, while both sets of parents
are asking for a better-behaving child, they are different "customers" holding different viewpoints and will need different
"sales pitches" if treatment is to succeed. Whatever the therapist will be instructing the different sets of parents to do, he
will frame the instructions to Set A as "therapeutic for the
child" and to Set B as "helping to establish appropriate parental
control."

Whereas conventional psychotherapy places importance
on listening for the underlying meaning of what the patient
says, we emphasize the importance of listening to the exact
wording of patients' remarks, because it is in the specific wording that they indicate their positions.

A patient may not initially give a clear indication of his
position about the problem. His phrasing is vague, or it contains
mixtures of seemingly contradictory views—"He was manipulative even with the therapist we sent him to." In such cases, a
definite position can often be elicited by a question: "You have
been filling me in on the problem and how it has gone; it would
help me further if you could give me your best guess as to *why*
the problem exists." Or "How do you explain this problem's
arising and persisting in the way it has?" In either case, the therapist is seeking the client's beliefs about the problem and, therefore, his position.

Determining a patient's position does not require great
concentration or breathless waiting for some hidden clue to appear, since the most useful positions are those that are strongly
held. These are likely to be expressed over and over in the
course of discussion. A therapist would have to actively disre-
gard such messages to miss them:

> "I think it best if I begin by telling you when I
> *first started having trouble.* I hadn't *even* gotten out
> of high school when I began having difficulty, and I

don't think I've been free of it *ever since.* It *got worse* in my senior year, and by the time I started college I *had to see a therapist.* I worked with him for *four years* but had to stop when I graduated and came up here. Then *I got into treatment* with Dr. Miller in the city and worked with him for *three years. He* then *felt it would be better* if I cut down to seeing him *only once a week.* That *seemed* to work OK for a while, but then I *fell apart* and *wound up hospitalized* for *two months* at . . ." ("I see myself as fragile and am pessimistic about ever getting over this trouble. In any case, it is a very serious problem and one that, even if it can be resolved, will take a very long time.")

"We are so *distraught* over John's *depression.* We *got him a bicycle,* hoping that he might help him *get out of the house* and be with other boys, but he hardly ever used it. Then we signed him up for *dance lessons,* figuring that if he got over his *shyness* he wouldn't be depressed, but he never went and we felt it *best not to push him.* We have *tried every way* to let him know *we care* about him. My husband took up fishing just so he *could take John on camping trips,* and we *make it a point to set aside at least one day a week* when we will do *whatever it is he would like.* But none of this has helped." ("We see John as seriously ill, and there is no sacrifice too great if it will help.")

"He keeps *putting me down,* especially in front of our friends, and so I am *constantly humiliated.* One time I *couldn't take it anymore,* and I walked out of the restaurant and drove home. *You know what he did?* He just stayed at a friend's house, rented a car, and *came rolling home* the next night *acting as if nothing happened.* That really *drove me wild.* I'm *climbing the walls,* and he just *sits there smoking that goddam pipe* of his." ("I want some respect from him, but, equally, I am furious and am aching to get one-up on him.")

"As I told you, it is very important for me to deal with this problem. Now, I'm going to have some *difficulty setting up another appointment* unless you see people at night. In fact, I was *lucky to be able to see you today,* and it was only possible because there was some screw-up at work, which left me with a free hour. But, obviously, I can't depend on that, and *what makes it worse is that I have to travel a lot,* and I can be sent on a trip on very short notice. So we could set up another appointment, although I might not be able to give you more than a *couple of hours' notice* when I have to *cancel* it, if that's OK. Or how about *if I called you* when I found I was going to be free and *if you had time* I could come right in?" ("While I have said it is very important to resolve my problem, I am in no rush; at the very least, the affairs of everyday life take precedence over working my problem out.")

Types of Positions

The positions that have a significant bearing on treatment fall into a rather narrow range. To begin with, people will either define themselves as the patients or they will define someone else—usually a family member—as the patient. If they define someone else as the patient, they will present themselves either as benevolently concerned about a person who is "sick" or as victimized by a person who is "bad."

Whether the client identifies himself as the patient or not, he will either take the position that the problem is a distinctly painful one, in which change is pressingly important, or he will take the position that the state of affairs is undesirable but not particularly uncomfortable and that change is not needed or, at least, not urgently needed.

Most often, the latter position is taken by an individual who is coming into therapy under duress or coercion; for example, an offender ordered to get treatment by the court as a condition of his probation, an "alcoholic" husband threatened with divorce by his wife "if you don't get some help," a child exhibiting behavior of concern to others, or most "schizophrenics."

Further, whatever the problem or whoever is defined as the patient, people will either convey a position of pessimism about resolution of the problem, or they will convey that the problem, while difficult, can be dealt with. In contrast to the patient who takes a pessimistic position regarding his problem, others may take not simply a more hopeful view but one of the converse of pessimism, a grandiose expectation about what one can and should accomplish—for example, "full self-actualization" or a life completely free from the fetters of everyday cares. While this position could be included in the dimension of pessimism/optimism, we have placed it in a separate category since it is characteristic of a special group of patients who have become casualties of the paradoxical injunction "You *must* be free!"

As for the therapy itself, patients will usually take one of three positions: They are to be the passive recipients of the therapist's wisdom and advice; or, conversely, they are to take active charge of the treatment, using the therapist as a passive sounding board; or, one hopes, they are there to get help through a mutual activity and responsiveness between themselves and the therapist. On another dimension of activity, patients will view the therapy process either as one requiring considerable discussion and insight ("I don't understand why . . .") or as one requiring some action on their part ("I don't know what to do when . . ."). This latter position is often attended by an additional position that resolution of the problem will be arrived at rationally or through "common sense," while others will indicate that the problem will be resolved by magical or unexpected means. These are really versions of the general themes that things occur through deliberation or spontaneity.

Finally, certain personal values can have a direct bearing on treatment and, when noticed, can be used to expedite "selling." For example, some patients see themselves as extraordinary and rising above common considerations; they are therefore motivated by a challenge, a dare. Others, instead, are intimidated by the fear of standing out and would shrink from

a challenge but welcome a task that is *apparently* small and un-
obtrusive. Some individuals will indicate that they see themselves as "caring" or "nurturing" and will be motivated to
undertake tasks framed as self-sacrificing yet constructive, rather than tasks framed as "You've got to think of yourself."

As mentioned before, positions about the problem can
overlap with positions regarding the treatment process itself. A
patient expressing pessimism about his problem is, at one and
the same time, expressing pessimism about the course, duration,
and outcome of treatment. However, we believe that further
discussion of attitudes toward treatment is important, so that
the therapist can enhance the progress of treatment by avoiding
costly pitfalls.

Probably the principal position regarding treatment is
whether the individual is defining himself as a client at all. This
does not mean whether he defines himself as the patient or not.
While we have been using "client" and "patient" as interchange-
able from the therapist's viewpoint, a distinction is necessary in
this specific context. A "client" in our usage here is an individual who is actively seeking help from a therapist; he is a "complainant." "Patient" here refers to the individual the complainant defines as the deviant or troubled person, either himself or
another. Thus, one can define himself as a client even though he
is coming in complaining about the behavior of another, whom
he identifies as the "patient." Indeed, this is most often the
case when parents seek the help of a therapist for their child.
Defining oneself as a client means that one is seriously interested in change and relief from the complaint, whether that
complaint is about oneself or about another. In its essence, such
a definition includes three elements: (1) "I have been struggling
with a problem that significantly bothers me." (2) "I have failed
to resolve it with my own efforts." (3) "I need your help in resolving it." One cannot expect most clients to state it that clearly and succinctly, however. Usually, it is conveyed in the narra-
tion of the problem and of the efforts fruitlessly made to resolve
it, or in response to comments by the therapist: "Well, I've
really been very depressed for some time now. I think it began
four months ago. At first, I just tried to shrug it off, but it got

worse and worse no matter how hard I tried to shake it and bring myself out of it. Well, last week I really got scared. I found myself starting to think about how I could do away with myself, and that shook me up. I realized how bad off I'd gotten, so I finally talked to my cousin, who'd gone through something similar. He said he had seen you and that you helped him a lot, so I called you the next day." In just these initial comments, the speaker has identified himself as a client and, additionally, as a patient.

Whether a person defines himself as a client or not can be of prime importance, since the nonclient is essentially not interested in changing the state of affairs, even if he is registering a complaint. He is not all that discomforted by the problem or, if he is, does not believe he has run the full gamut of his own resources to solve it or, even if he is at his wit's end to resolve it, does not believe that psychotherapy is the appropriate alternative. Most often, the individual taking this position is in the therapist's office under duress from someone else—his parents, spouse, the courts, or his grown children.

The therapist will find that he has considerable difficulty in getting the nonclient down to the business of treatment. Responses to questions will characteristically be sullenly terse or, conversely, amiable ramblings about broad generalities of philosophies, current events, and the like. In either case, the therapist will have to work harder to try to get any useful information. Concomitantly, setting appointments will be difficult: "I won't be able to make this time anymore. Do you have appointments in the evening?" or "I don't want to set another appointment right now. I just wanted to see how we would get along. I need to check out a couple of other therapists I'm seeing next week." (For further discussion of recognition of and interventions with the nonclient, see Chapters Two and Four.)

One other position is important to identify and deal with as early as possible in treatment. The client may be truly bothered by his problem, at his wit's end, and actively seeking therapy. However, he has such strong notions about the proper structure of treatment that he is disinclined to allow the therapist to determine fundamental procedural decisions; instead, he attempts to impose on the therapist conditions that, if permitted, would prevent any likelihood of resolution of his problem. In essence, whatever his intentions, he is attempting to tie the therapist's hands: "I need to make some decision about my marriage, but I want to make it clear that under no circumstances is my wife to know I'm seeing you." Or "Since my problem is one of having repressed my feelings, I won't be able to work with you unless I have assurance I can express my feelings as fully as I feel them. My previous therapist encouraged me to do that, and I certainly will pay for any breakage in your office." Or "I can see you only maybe once a month." As with the position of nonclient, there are alternatives to dismissing these clients or suffering through an impossible arrangement. These alternatives are dealt with in Chapter Two.

Utilizing Patient Position

After the therapist has determined a client's position regarding his problem and regarding therapy, how does the therapist make use of this information? First of all, for the purpose of brevity of treatment, the therapist does not want to make comments that will engender resistance on the part of the patient—unless as part of a planned stratagem. Second, also for brevity's sake, he will want to maximize a patient's compliance with suggestions. Patient position can be utilized to achieve both these aims; but, while achieving the former will keep the therapist out of trouble, the second consideration is most relevant for making headway toward resolution of the problem. For that reason, we will have more to say on this latter aim.

Avoiding Resistance. A therapist can engender resistance by making comments that are inflammatory to patients or that reduce the credibility of his ideas. For example, if the patient expresses an attitude of pessimism ("The problem has been going on for so long and previous treatment has not helped, but my doctor says that you have been able to help a lot of people with my kind of problem") the therapist can produce significant resistance by responding in any way that indicates a position of optimism: "You sound a little discouraged about yourself and about previous therapy, but I don't think you need to feel that way. Perhaps the first task of therapy should focus on why you feel so discouraged." Despite the positive intention behind these comments, they run counter to the client's position of pessimism, and one might predict that they will impede the client's cooperation and a successful outcome in treatment, especially if the client has already been discouraged by previous therapists who began treatment on a positive, optimistic note, only to terminate with no improvement. The therapist could stay out of hot water if he said nothing in reply, but such silence might be interpreted as agreement that he has "worked wonders." In any case, it is always more useful to respond—but in a way that promotes favorable movement; for that purpose, the therapist will want to match his comment with that of the patient: "I can certainly understand your hope that I will be of help to you, but considering all that you have been through and the failure of previous efforts to help, I think it much more appropriate that you start off treatment with me on the basis of skepticism rather than blind optimism. After all is said and done, results are the only thing one can hang one's hat on." By stating this position, the therapist can, paradoxically, lessen the patient's pessimism, since he will be implying that he recognizes the patient's discouragement and its validity and that he will not patronize him through false hope. Moreover, although the therapist's words are pessimistic or at least cautionary, his allusion to the possibility of *results* is, on an implicit and therefore unchallengeable level, optimistic.

In other kinds of interchanges, the therapist can reduce his credibility by unwittingly making comments that are inflammatory:

Husband (in conjoint session with wife): That kid of ours is the bane of our existence. If it weren't for him, we'd have no problems. We have a good marriage, a beautiful home, and enjoy many activities, but he is driving us to distraction.

Th: Well, John. You say you have a good marriage. Yet Sandy has said you sleep in separate bedrooms, hardly go anywhere together, and don't even have normal disagreements. It seems to me that your complaining so much about your son might be obscuring the problems that exist in the marriage.

This comment is likely to provoke the husband. First of all, he has said, and in front of his wife, that he regards the marriage as a good one; the attribution the therapist is making implies that he is either lying or glossing over the obvious difficulties. Moreover, since his principal stated concern is his son, not the marriage, the therapist's comment can suggest that his complaint is not legitimate and that the therapist is siding with the son and wife against him. Again, the therapist can stay out of hot water by not commenting on the marriage—at least, not at that point in treatment. Better yet, he can use the father's position to enhance cooperation: "Especially since you do have a good marriage, then I would expect that you will do all in your power to help resolve the difficulty with your son, so that you and your wife can more thoroughly enjoy your marriage."

To avoid creating unnecessary patient resistance, then, a therapist should accept the client's statements, recognize the values they represent, and avoid making inflammatory or noncredible comments. Naturally, being clear about what *not* to say will make it easier to know what to say, with whatever timing and pacing the therapist chooses. At times, simple nodding will convey acceptance of the patient's statement, and nothing further need be done, at least at that time.

Enhancing Patient Cooperation. At the phase of treatment we are concerned with, the therapist will have formulated some task or action, which, if taken by the patient, should increase the chances for resolution of the problem. He now has to present this task or action to the patient in a way consistent with the position that the patient has been conveying. Suppose, for example, the clients are parents of a child who is grossly misbehaving at home—throwing temper tantrums, being disorderly in his personal routines, being uncooperative about household chores, and the like. However, they do not view this behavior as defiance or simple misconduct but as a manifestion of some deep psychological problem: "He has poor self-esteem" or "He is troubled by something he can't talk to us about." Because of

mind stray to the pleasures of driving or traveling. I think at least a half hour each day should be put into this exercise. [Should the patient return and say, as hoped for, that he was impatient with the therapist's slow pace—for example, that he couldn't resist the temptation to turn the motor on—then the therapist will want to persist with his "restraining" tack. Step by step, all driving can be stated as restraints: "I want you to drive *no more than* around the corner" or "I want you to drive *no further than* the nearest store, and, regardless of how well you manage it, I want you to leave the car and walk back home."]

In cases where the patient's fear is of rejection by the opposite sex, he is asked to maximize the chances of rejection deliberately. He may be asked to go some place where people meet—a bar, dance hall, or skating rink—and to pick out the most desirable looking woman and to approach her with the simple introduction "I would like to get to know you better but I am very shy talking with women." He is also told that under the circumstances, he is likely to be rejected—after all, he has picked out a woman who can be choosy, and his opener is absurdly simple. Even if by some chance he is not rejected, he is instructed not to take her out or see her again, since the prime purpose of the assignment is to make him more immune to the impact of rejection—not to meet women!

The common thread in strategies of resolving fear/avoidance problems, then, is to expose the patient to the feared task while restraining him from successfully completing it. As explained, this common strategy can be used as a general guideline, since the patient's more frequent "solution" is to avoid the task while pushing himself to master it.

3. Attempting to Reach Accord Through Opposition

The problems connected with this solution involve conflict in an interpersonal relationship that centers on issues requiring mutual cooperation. These problems would include marital fights, conflicts between parents and their rebellious children or teenagers, employee disputes, and problems of grown children with their elderly parents.

Rarely are both parties in such altercations customers for treatment. Usually, the therapist will be contacted by the person who feels that the legitimacy of his or her position is threatened or denied by the other party. It may be the parent who feels the child does not respect his or her authority or the spouse who feels "put down" by his or her mate. Although the complainant will attempt to coerce the offending party to seek help or join them in treatment, these efforts usually fail, or, at best, result in a single visit by the "offending" party.

Complainants with these problems engage in the attempted solution of haranguing the other party to comply with their demands for specific behaviors, and, even more importantly, demand that the other party treat them with the respect, care, or deference they feel is due. In short, the attempted solution takes the form of demanding that the other party treat them as "one up."

This form of problem solving simply provokes the very behavior the complainant wishes to eliminate, whether the demand for "one-upness" is phrased as being right or being in charge, and whether it is pursued by threats, force, or by logical argument.

One way to interdict this solution is by getting the complainant to take a "one-down" position—that is, a position of weakness. The required shift in the attempted solution is difficult for the complainant to make, given the intensity of the interpersonal struggle. He will probably view taking a one-down position as weakness, knuckling under, or a final step in abdicating his right as a parent or spouse. However, such a reversal is usually required in these cases because if the complainant simply stopped his attempted solution with no explanation, the other party would be likely to regard this as simply more of the same: Instead of complaining, he is silently biding his time. Consequently, the other party probably would maintain a defensive stance and draw the complainant back into using his problem-maintaining solution.

Since the required shift in the attempted solution is usually a difficult shift for the client, intervening in such problems demands that the therapist be more concerned with the framing or "selling" aspect of the intervention than with identifying the specific action the client needs to take, which may be evident. In general, the client will need an explanation that can allow him to make requests comfortably in a nonauthoritarian manner, such as "I would appreciate it if you would . . . ." rather than "You've got to . . . ." or "It's the very least you can do."

In the area of childrearing, especially with teenagers, parents often attempt to bring about compliance by overstatement of their power: "It's our house, and as long as you are living here, you will have to abide by our rules!" "Well, too bad, but you can't go out now; if you do, I will ground you for two weeks!" Usually, the parents either cannot or will not enforce such threats with real consequences. Whatever actions they do take are apt to be small, such as withholding allowances for a week or two. In our experience, empty threats are both provocative and easily recognized as "paper tigers." Interestingly, many such parents do not make use of the actual power they have to impose sanctions, withhold important favors, and so on.

In these cases, intervening actually starts when the therapist asks to meet with the parents alone first. The format implicitly confirms the parents as the complainants; at the same time, it places the parents in the position of consulting the therapist about the management of their child. This is in marked distinction from conventional treatment, where the therapist will often start with the child, who is made the major focus of treatment, even if the parents attend subsequent sessions.

Though the therapist recognizes the provocative effect the parents have on their child, he is not likely to tell them that, as such a statement is likely to antagonize them and reduce their cooperation. The parents' frame of reference is that they are appropriately insisting on compliance in keeping with their legitimate position as the authorities in the home: "He must realize we are his parents and we have a right to expect he will keep his room neat." Instead, the therapist will reframe the situation with their child in such a way that they will be able to take a one-down stance while feeling that they are still in an authoritative position.

One useful framing for such problems is to explain to the

parents that the child never really pays attention to what they
are telling him. The parents have become so predictable that the
child simply tunes them out. If they wish to get through to
him, they must gain his attention, and one way of doing this is
by becoming *unpredictable*. Consider the following example
where this framing was used as a means of influencing the parent to engage in one-down behavior.

Th: I have no quarrel with what you have been asking of your
son. If anything, you are asking too little. But be that as it may,
the more important thing is that you underestimate how predictable you are to your son. After the first word or two, he can
predict what you will say next and he just tunes out. From
what I have observed, you never let him down in this respect.
No, if you are to get through to him, you must first get his attention, but this will require unpredictability on your part.

Pt: Well, I don't know how we could be unpredictable [Thus
indicating an acceptance of the need to shift but asking *how* it
can be done] Maybe we could . . .

Th: Well, think a bit. Let's see. When he is leaving the house
in the evening, I believe you characteristically say, "Remember.
You are supposed to be back by 10:00. You make sure you get
back by then. We don't want you out any later." Would there
be some way of saying something about hours but which would
be uncharacteristic and therefore unpredictable?

Pt: How about if we asked him what time he thinks is fair to
come home?

Th: That would be different, but what if he said "midnight."
No, I don't think that would work, but you have given me an
idea. Would it be uncharacteristic of you to say "We'd appreciate it if you were in by 10:00, but we can't make you come
home by then"?

Pt: Yes [laughing], that certainly would be different for us.
But how would he react?

Th: Well, you really don't know until you try it. Would there
be anything lost in trying it out this week?

Or, in a more complex case, the framing used focused on the mother preparing her child for adult life.

Observer: [Entering room] I came in because Dr. X [the case therapist, who has been struggling with the parents] is trying to convey . . . We had, as you can imagine, a heavy conference, in which we beat him soundly around the head and shoulders. And I think it was unfair to try to ask him to relate, as accurately as he would need to, the conversation among several of us in there about some points. And in your comment—what you just said—I assume that you might not have been making it as clear as it should be. At the risk of being repetitive with some of it, the point that we were making is that in Jill's irresponsible handling of herself—at home, in the community, at school—and to the best of our judgment, it is on the basis of what Dr. X has been saying is that she has been operating, and I think still operating, on a four-year-old notion that she can do what she pleases because, no matter what happens, Mommy will protect her. And therefore, she does not have to watch her step. "Mommy will pluck me from harm's way at the eleventh hour." This is a dangerous psychology to operate on when you are not four years old, and instead when you are at her age, and increasingly so every day, and quite correctly, he's giving us a prime example: "You've been arrested, you've been incarcerated in the Juvenile Hall, you've had a hearing, you've been on home arrest, and you are now to go into a court for a final disposition, and you giggle." This is a four-year-old psychology. She maintains that illusion—that you can and will rescue her—by snookering you into taking a "good parent," restrictive, reminding, and reasonable role. And if you persist in that, we can guarantee your kid will go down the drain.

M: So what you're, then, in essence—excuse me, I hope I'm not interrupting—but then, what you're telling me in essence is that I'm going to kind of have to just—hands-off policy.

Ob: No. No. Worse than that. She needs to be appropriately and constructively frightened—frightened because it is an important realization that she needs to come to, which is that the cord has been cut. "Mama can't protect me." I am on my own more than I, and probably more than you, realized. And the court has realized. They are naive." Go to school and do well. Or we will send you someplace where we will make you do well. That is naive. But to be frightened by the constructive realization, "I've got to watch my step. Mama can't watch it for me. Mama can't protect me." Not Mama *won't*. "Mama *can't* protect me."

M: Uh-huh. But how do I go about getting her in to that position?

Ob: OK. Believe it or not, it would be . . . Let me start in general and say something more specific. It would be to be "a bad parent." If you want to help her and to arrive as quickly as possible at this most necessary realization, it'll be that you will be coming on with her, handling things—it is not a hands-off policy—handling things in a way that one would assume a bad parent would do. For example, rather than "Do you have homework? Did you finish your homework" all of which reassures her "You're gonna protect me," instead it would not be hands off, but "I don't know whether you have homework or not, but there's a neat TV program on tonight. Why don't you come in and watch it?" By the way, don't make the mistake of . . . I think you said that you're the enforcer right now, at least, and Jill doesn't know that.

M: Uh, she . . . I probably didn't put that quite as well as she does realize that for the time being, at least for the next two weeks, that, yes, I will be the total enforcer. After she is assigned to her regular probation officer, then it will be more up to him. But what she doesn't realize is that her everyday living at home, that I would be the one that would, you know, as she would put it, would squeal on her.

Ob: She learned that the first five minutes she was in Juvenile Hall.

M: No, she hasn't let on! But I'm sure you're probably right.

Ob: That's what she learned in the sixth minute: You don't let on.

M: I never thought about that.

Ob: There is a very rapid exchange of information in Juvenile Hall. So that's why you've got to talk about it.

M: Yeah.

Ob: OK, you are expected to be the enforcer; she knows that. You can help her go down the drain by being a good enforcer. You can help her to, hopefully, handle herself better, and more maturely and self-controlled, if you're a rotten enforcer. A "bad mother" enforcer. You're careless about her; you forget; you just don't even bother. "I know you know I went over and spoke to one of my forbidden friends. I suppose you'll probably have to tell my probation officer." "Probably, but I don't know. As a matter of fact, Jill, I'm not gonna spell it out, but there are a number of things I'm not too happy with about the court and the judge. But I'm not gonna tell you where I found my differences. I'm not too happy with them. Sometimes I think they're full of nonsense." I'm a very bad citizen. A bad mother. Right.

M: Well, that would be . . . I will do it because I think your suggestion is great.

Ob: It's going to be very, very hard to do, and you'll fight against this role so different from what you're used to. You raise your kids, and in raising them it is appropriate to guide them, control them, discipline them, and protect them. And with a four-year-old you can do it. A four-year-old is intimidated. And everybody in the community will support you: "What are you doing here? You go right on home." And the kid goes trotting on home. You can bust up a bunch of four-year-olds, eight-year-olds, easy. They start getting into the teens, pre-teens, they're thick as thieves: they've got peer support, they've got dough, and they've been encouraged to try their wings—this whole idea of leading into adulthood. It's that difficult business of shifting gears to no longer protecting your child, with the unhappy realization you *can't*. Where is she now? Where is she right now? Is she at school? How do you know that?

M: Home.

Ob: Home?

M: She's supposed to be home.

Ob: How do you know that?

M: I don't.

Ob: OK. An eight-year-old, you can say, "You stay home till I get back," and they'll stay. They're intimidated. But it's that difficult realization that I . . . You don't have to stop caring about your kid—you'll always care—but because you care it means the requirement of shifting to getting them to protect themselves. I've reached the end of my capability to protect them. Now it's a question of getting them to protect them-selves. And in a sense, home turns into a survival training camp.

M: Yes, it does.

Ob: The troops don't survive . . . You want to be nice to your troops, so why put them through the rigors, and the risks for that matter, of the . . . Why have them crawl through barbed wire? . . . It's dangerous. And then you send them out into bat-tle? They get slaughtered.

M: That's true.

Ob: So home is a survival training camp for a lot of teens, but especially teens who, like Jill, have not been handling them-selves well. They've got some lessons to learn, the most impor-tant of which is "The cord's been cut, kid." And you know that every time your mom comes on like she's incompetent, forget-ful, irresponsible . . . So you'd better not depend on her to pro-tect you.

M: Yeah. I really do understand, and I do see the logic in it. It makes a lot of sense to me. I will do it.

Ob: Well, OK. Be prepared; it's gonna be difficult. You'll be fighting against your instincts . . . And Jill also will make it hard for you by—At times—I think it would be best to anticipate—by trying to snooker you back into the "You can't" position. "Have you done this, and have you done that?" She'll try to snooker you back into that; she'll probably be good at it. So why don't you just study how she tries to do it, and if you can, don't get snookered back into it.

M: Yeah.

Th: My colleagues in the back room pointed out that this may not work—this approach may not work—the first time. It may not work the second time. You may say something about watching TV and not doing the homework, and she may just give up the homework altogether. And that this may take five or six times; it will take some time to change.

Ob: Oh, yes. I hope I didn't convey, you know, an overnight change or success with it.

M: Oh, I realize that.

Ob: You know, it's the starting of and the persistence with a tack—a fundamental tack—that will take some time.

M: No, I realize that, believe me. It's taken her fifteen years to get where she is. I do know it's not going to be an overnight change.

Sometimes the parents will not budge from their one-up position because they are fearful of "completely losing control" over their child. The kind of framing described above may not reassure them that they are maintaining a controlling position. In such cases, they can be offered a "magic sword"; that is, the therapist suggests they have at their disposal a more powerful means of bringing about compliance, of which they have never availed themselves, the use of unpredictable and unannounced consequences. However, the "magic sword" requires a one-down verbal stance to be effective. In brief, this tactic, called "benevolent sabotage," is an appeal to the parents to use actual consequences instead of harangues; these consequences are to occur in an "accidental" way, and the parents are to apologize for them if questioned by the child: "Oh, I'm terribly sorry there were crumbs in your bed last night. I must have been having breakfast and walking around with the toast when I straightened up your room. I'll try not to let it happen again."

With some parents, the intervention can be as simple as repetitively defining one-up as the weak position and one-down as the strong position. They are accused of taking too "weak" a position with their child and instructed, instead, to take the one-down, or "strong," position. Such an uncomplicated tactic is not likely to work with most parents, but the therapist can use it appropriately with those parents who say they are at their absolute wit's end and are willing to try anything that has any chance of success, as in the following example of the parents of a difficult, provocative teenage girl:

Th: So will you bring me up to date, please?

M: Well, we've just had all kinds of excitement—just doing what you said, you know. I've had Suzie in tears all week—total frustration, you know. An example is a couple days ago where she said to me, "Is a sweater enough to wear to school today?" So I said, "Well it's awfully cold, Suzie. A coat might be better." And she said, "But it might get hot this afternoon; then I'd have to carry it home." So I said, "Then probably a sweater would be fine." So she said, "You make me sick." She says, "I'm never speaking to you again," and left.

Th: Which means what to you?

M: I don't know, it just means I won't argue with her about anything, and that makes her mad.

Father: She [mother] used to say, "You wear the coat to school. It's freezing cold, and if it gets warm you carry it home and that's it." "Well, I don't know why I have to carry it if I don't want to. I'm the one that's gonna get cold," and she'd argue about it. But now, when she [mother] says something, she'll say, "Well, I'll think about it, Suzie. I'll see." And stuff like that.

M: Well, like the sewing machine, for instance . . .

F: She just goes—She just, like, she don't know what to say next 'cause no one will fight with her. You know, she tries all kinds of maneuvers to get into arguments. And when no one will argue with her, she just gets frustrated and don't know what to do, you know.

Th: So, in this past week, you have tried . . . You made a good job out of not giving information. It would be much more powerful, of course, if you were unable to give information simply because you are so depressed and upset . . . I would like you to take an even more powerful position. And this may sound absurd to you, because that more powerful position that I would like you to take would be one of seeming helplessness, and being very upset.

In marital problems, the complainant will usually try to wrest consideration from the spouse through complaint rather than request. What is worse, the complaints are often put in a rhetorical form that is particularly incendiary: "Why is it you can be considerate to any damned stranger but not to me or the children?" "When are you going to take me into consideration instead of thinking of your own comfort all the time?" When requests are made, they are often vague or equivocal. "You know, it would be nice if you took me out to dinner once in a while." "I don't need any jewelry, but it would be nice if you got me something anyhow." The therapist will want to interdict the one-up demandingness and the failure to make requests explicit. In a nutshell he will want the complainant to frame requests concretely and specifically: "I'd appreciate it (or, "I'd really love it") if we could go out to dinner tomorrow night." Influencing the complainant spouse to adopt that form usually requires some framing; otherwise the spouse will simply view it as knuckling under or taking too supplicating a position. The framing most likely to be accepted is one that affords the client the *sense* that they will be in a one-up position in relation to their spouse. The following is a simulated example of such a framing:

Th: You know, it's interesting. You say you would like more consideration from your husband, yet you let him off the hook in the way you convey that need.

Pt: But I don't. I remind him how he's treated me, how most of the men he knows treat their wives much better. I have made it very plain.

Th: That's precisely it! That very effort conveys a desperation, a desperation he is likely to read as your seeing him as your sun and moon and stars; that you, somehow, will wither if he doesn't shine his attentions on you. This puts him in too important a position, one in which he can feel that any crumbs he throws your way should be sufficient.

Pt: Yes. The few times he has done anything for me he acts as if he gave me his right arm.

Th: If you are serious about hoping to change the role you've been playing, it will require your getting him off the pedestal you have helped create. And that, mainly, will require making your requests more casual. However, to be able to do that will require enough dignity on your part so that he can recognize he isn't the center of your universe. If you are up to it, you will probably find yourself expressing requests more casually—something like "I'd appreciate it if . . ." and then making the request specific so he can't hedge about it, claiming he was unclear what it was you wanted.

There is a special, triangular, context in which, for example, one parent is in conflict with a teenage child, and the other parent tries to be a peacekeeper. Almost any comment by either of the opponents, but especially any comment expressing disagreement, will rapidly flare up into a stormy battle and will end with one or both parties stomping out of the room. The problem is unwittingly maintained by the peacekeeper. She would like to see a better relationship between the two warring parties and is personally discomforted by the noise and rancor created during the fights. She attempts to resolve differences by "reasoning" with one or both parties, most often shortly after a blowup. The reasoning, instead of calming the waters, is actually inflammatory. The peacekeeper tells the other parent he has been too impatient or harsh with their child or has not adequately recognized the child's needs or position, thus taking that parent to task and, unwittingly, indicating a coalition between the child and herself. To the child, the peacekeeper explains that the other parent "really loves you" and asks the child for patience or forebearance. This, too, has an inflammatory effect because it implies criticism of the child and a coalition between the mother and father.

However well meant, such peacekeeping efforts further polarize the relationship between the combatants, while convincing the peacekeeper that the situation requires expert help. In most cases of this sort, the peacekeeper, who is the chief complainant, usually urges the therapist to bring in the warring parties and to serve as a more expert peacekeeper; that is, to do more of the same, but better.

Obviously, the therapist will want to avoid this invitation, and will need to frame the treatment as requiring the peacekeeper's active participation "at least in the beginning." A temptation to avoid is simply to tell the "peacekeeper" to "butt out and let them settle it themselves." Even if the complainant should agree to that, she would soon find it hard to implement since the battles between the spouse and child are apt to reach levels too noisy and frightening for her to ignore: objects thrown, pushing or hitting, and so on. Rather, the therapist will want to promote and use her position of intermediary, but in a different way.

Th: Well, you can try to stay out of it, but I don't think that will work. I think they can outwait you. You see, they depend on the fact that you have always stepped in and rescued them. In any case, you said you've tried staying out of it but that hasn't worked.

Pt: That's true. I've left the house, but you can hear that yelling and screaming all the way down the block. I just had to come back. But I really am so tired of getting caught in the middle.

Th: I can understand that, but you can only get out of the middle if and when your husband and your child no longer need you to serve that function.

Pt: But I don't see that happening. They just fight.

Th: They can continue to fight because they count on your being a *reasonable* go-between. You are the voice of reason, and they, incorrectly, assume that you can do their negotiating for them. In that way they avoid using and developing their own resources for negotiation. What it will take to change this is something that might still strike you as strange, that of becoming an *unreasonable* negotiator.

Pt: Unreasonable, how?

Th: You see, when you go to them and point out the unreasonableness of their actions, they do not hear what you are saying but only that you yourself are taking the trouble to be reasonable. They depend on your being reasonable with the other one in the fight and thus being the more level-headed spokesman for each of them. However, if you were to convey that you might not be that level-headed, they might start to feel they need to do their own negotiating. That unreasonable position can best be conveyed by not only commiserating with each of their own positions but even taking it further than they have —perhaps to an absurd point, so that they each have to become reasonable with you, pointing out that you are going too far. Obviously, if you could get either of them to do that you would know you are having a beneficial effect. I would have to leave the wording up to you, but it would be some form of "I can't say I blame you for getting so angry with him. As a matter of fact, I don't think you went far enough."

Here, the therapist has redefined the peacekeeper's role as one of intermediary and further defined it as a "reasonable" intermediary, a "reasonableness" that has a counterproductive outcome. If the patient accepts those redefinitions, the thrust of the strategy can be extended so that she no longer takes an inflammatory position with the contenders but commiserates with each of them. Commiseration has a more calming effect than opposition.

4. Attempting to Attain Compliance Through Voluntarism

This solution, a mirror image of attempting to achieve spontaneity through deliberateness, can be summed up in the statement "I would like him to do it but, even more, I want him to *want* to do it." It appears to reflect an abhorrence of asking something of another that might be distasteful or require some

effort or sacrifice. To ask for what one wants directly is seen as
dictatorial or a harmful intrusion into the other person's integ-
rity. It is as if the other person is regarded as fragile, as incapa-
ble of determining his own level of compliance, as someone who
cannot say "no"; therefore, paradoxically his "freedom" has to
be maintained by someone else. This confusion and contradic-
tion is illustrated by citing (also in *Change,* Chapter 6) the mental gyrations suffered by the mother whose eight-year-old boy is
not eager to do his homework and other chores:

> I think what I am trying to say is: I want Andy
> to learn to do things, and I want him to do things—
> but I want *him* to want to do them. I mean, he could
> follow orders blindly and not want to. I realize that I
> am making a mistake, I cannot pinpoint what I am
> doing wrong, but I cannot agree with dictating to him
> what to do—yet, if a child were to be put completely
> on his own like that, he would eventually be mired
> down into a room this deep (referring to clothes,
> toys, etc., on the floor) or whatever—no, these are—
> there are two extremes. I want him to *want* to do
> things, but I realize it's going to be something that we
> have to *teach* him.

This troublesome paradox manifests itself in a number of
clinical forms—marital problems, childrearing problems, and
"schizophrenia."

For example, in what is commonly called "young adult
schizophrenia," a parent might be distressed by his son's bizarre
behavior, such as walking around the house clad only in under-
wear. He would like his son to put more clothes on and behave
normally, but the father will not simply ask him to do that. Instead, he will try to induce the son to do this as a "voluntary"
act: "I know you are feeling cold walking around like that and
I'm sure you would be more comfortable dressed warmer. But
of course, I don't want you to do that if you don't feel it's right
for you. You must decide that kind of thing for yourself." The
son could diminish the problem if he answered directly "Look,
if you're asking me to put on more clothes, forget it. I happen

to be quite comfortable this way, crazy as it may seem to you."
However, the problem will be escalated if the son's rejoinder—as
is likely—is as indirect as the parent's statement: "One has to do
what one has to do" (or more bizarre ripostes: "I think the
spirits are calling me").

In such a situation, what would otherwise be a simple request for compliance which might be responded to by a simple
statement of refusal (or even agreement) has, instead, become a
problem-engendering interchange: indirect request met by indirect refusal, each person convincing the other that directness
of address is futile. The more veiled or bizarre the refusal, the
more the parent is convinced of his son's fragility, thus escalat-
ing the felt need for indirectness in subsequent transactions.
That is, much of what is called schizophrenia can usefully be
viewed as a disease of overpoliteness on the participants' parts:
"I'm not really telling you what I want you to do." "OK, I'm
not really refusing either."

In some marital problems, the paradox is manifested in
the complaint "My husband ignores my needs—needs that he
should be aware of without my having to tell him. If I have to
tell him what I would like, it would be worse than no good,
since then, should he comply, he would be doing it only because I asked him and not because he *really* wanted to."

Finally, this solution is at play in all those problems
where person *A* has asked person *B* to perform some act or
make a decision, and when *B* resists the request, *A* attempts to
counter *B*'s resistance by pointing out what has been asked for
is only fair or reasonable. Thus, in effect, *A* asks *B* to stop complaining and resisting, and do what *A* wants voluntarily. In all of
these problems, the common thread involves one person attempting to gain compliance from another while denying that
compliance is being asked for.

The overall strategy for dealing with such problems is to
get the person who is asking for something to ask for it directly, even if the request is made arbitrarily. The problem for the
therapist in these cases is finding a framing that will influence
the client to make this shift.

For example, such clients are often motivated by the desire to be benevolent, a position which may be stated: "I don't want him to do it if he really isn't happy doing it." The therapist can utilize this position by redefining the patient's benevolence, his indirect requests, as *unwittingly* destructive, and conversely, by redefining what the client may regard as destructive, direct requests, as beneficial.

Th: [to parent] In putting together all the data, I believe that what lies at the heart of your son's poor adjustment is a fear that he is too powerful in making you and your wife feel guilty. Unfortunately, when you are careful and gentle with him, you unwittingly confirm this in his mind and your best intentions, therefore, are having a destructive effect. He needs to be reassured that he isn't that powerful, and you can convey that by making rather considerable demands on him and, if need be, imposing some consequences should he fail to oblige you.

The therapist can provide extra "persuasion" by saying that "Perhaps I am asking too much of you, but I only dared to ask because I have felt that you are willing to make sacrifices if that could benefit your son." Even further pressure can be applied: "Of course, it might be best not to bother with what I suggest. After all, your son has not been that rewarding to you and you are entitled to take the easy path by continuing what you have been doing, and let him pay the price of failure in his life."

Similarly, a husband's reticence to ask favors of his wife can be redefined as an "unwitting deprivation of the one thing she most needs from you, a sense of your willingness to take leadership."

5. Confirming the Accuser's Suspicions by Defending Oneself

In these problems, usually, one person suspects another of some act that both parties agree is wrong—infidelity, excessive drinking, delinquency, dishonesty. Typically, person *A* makes accusations about person *B*, and *B* responds by denying the accusations and defending himself. Unfortunately, *B*'s defense usually confirms A's suspicions (as in "the lady doth protest too much"). As a result, A continues his accusations, B strengthens his defense, and so on.

We have referred to this interactional pattern as the game of accuser/defender. It can be observed in marital problems ("I'm sure he is having an affair"), in childrearing problems ("We know she is getting into trouble"), and work-related difficulties ("We know he is drinking on the job").

The "game" would end if either party departed from his repetitive role. Sometimes this can be achieved by seeing the defender alone. The therapist explains that the accuser is the one who is mistaken or causing the problem, and the defender, who also wants the game to end, may be able to resolve the problem by taking unilateral action. However, this action will be difficult, because, in the therapist's opinion, the only way the accuser can gain insight into his mistaken accusation is for the defender to agree with the accusations, especially if this acceptance can be carried to an obviously absurd length.

For example, we treated an elderly couple who had been engaging in this game for over thirty years. She accused him of "not being any fun" and of having provided only a mediocre financial existence. He defended himself by claiming he had done the best he could. He had given up a profession in Europe to come to America and marry her, and she was unappreciative of the many sacrifices he had made for her.

After a few conjoint sessions for data collection and case planning, our major thrust of treatment was to see him alone and convince him to make two statements to his wife whenever she made accusations. First, he was to say, "You're right. I'm no fun. The doctor helped me to see it." Second, "They told me that I am too old to change." Naturally, we were ready to support this view if the wife inquired about our prognosis. However, this was not necessary. After a few rounds of accusation and agreement, the game ended.

The game of accuser/defender can also be ended by using an intervention called jamming. It is an intervention which is designed to reduce the information value of interpersonal communication, thereby making verbal exchanges between two par-

ties somewhat futile since there is no way of knowing if they
are *really* getting to the facts of the matter.

If, for example, a wife is accusing her husband of excessive drinking, which he is denying, the therapist can set the
stage for the jamming intervention by taking a nonaligned position: "My role here is not to play detective and determine
which one of you is right or wrong. My role is limited to aiding
both of you in your communication with each other since that
has, obviously, broken down. Therefore, I cannot concern myself with how much you really do or do not drink." If the patients do not vigorously object to this definition of the therapist's
role, he can begin jamming the "game."

Th [to husband] :   However much or little you drink, it would
be important in the final resolution of the problem that your
wife be much more perceptive about your level of drinking. I
believe she is not as accurate as she would hope to be, and I
need to test this out. And you will need to help her. This week,
I want you to randomize your drinking and, at the same time,
randomize your behavior. For example, on one night before
you come home, I want you to have only one drink but then
act drunk when you come in the door. On another night, do
just the reverse. And so forth. You are then to keep a record of
what you've drunk each day and how you acted. [Turning to
the wife] Your task is to see how perceptive you are in looking
behind his surface behavior to assess, as best you can, exactly
how much he has drunk. You should also be keeping your own
"scorecard." I don't want you to compare scorecards: we will
do that when you come in next week.

By asking them to perform this test, the therapist has put
the couple into an interesting position vis-à-vis each other. The
task introduces a note of uncertainty about the husband's
"drunken behavior." Is he really drunk or just acting on the
therapist's orders? It is now very difficult for the accuser to
confront her husband. Concomitantly, since he is to deliberately fake intoxication, he is no longer under the same pressure to
defend himself. He has license to indict himself, but the indict-

ment cannot be relied on. In this sense, the therapist has "jammed" the game of accuser/defender.

Jamming can be used to solve other problems, and the basic strategy is the same. In a conjoint session, the "accused" is asked to do something, but the doing is framed in a way that makes the actual execution and report unreliable. For example, a teenager accused as "untrustworthy" might be asked to do something his parents would heartily approve of but not to tell them what it is. The parents, on the other hand, are instructed to try to worm out of him what good thing he did "through any means, direct or subtle." Finally, the teenager is told that if he feels he can no longer hold out and is on the verge of telling them, as a last resort he is to make up a lie by saying he did something bad. Thus, if the parents start to question the boy and he says he was reprimanded by the teacher that day, they do not know if their son is telling the truth or following the therapist's instructions, and therefore there is no point in pressing him for a confession.

One additional application: It is not uncommon in the problem of anorgasmia for a husband to check his wife's level of arousal during intercourse or inquire if she reached orgasm. In our view, these well-meant efforts simply put more pressure on the wife to reach orgasm. Jamming can be effective in interdicting such efforts.

The therapist can begin by telling the wife in the presence of her husband that one aspect of the problem has to do with her need to be more aware of her feelings and sensations, particularly during sexual intercourse. Therefore, as an initial step in dealing with the problem, in any subsequent sexual encounter she is to simply notice her bodily sensations, *regardless of how much or how little* pleasure she may experience. And since this process should not be interfered with, her husband is not to inquire as to her level of arousal. However, if for some reason he forgets this instruction, thereby interfering with the treatment, she is always to tell him the same thing: "I haven't felt a thing." This injunction makes his checking irrelevant since he can't get an answer that gives him any real information. Simultaneously, it frees the wife from his implicitly pressuring her to reach orgasm.

II. General Interventions

There are times when the therapist may want to convey some position of a general sort to set the stage for a subsequent, more specific, intervention. Or he may want to use such a position to determine if this alone is sufficient to resolve the problem, even though it would not have involved a specific directive to the client. Taking such "positions" constitutes intervention, and therefore we include them here because of their wide utility even though they are not dependent on the particular problem or solution the client is caught up in.

1. Go Slow

Of all interventions, perhaps the injunction to the patient to go slow in his resolution of the problem is the tactic we use most frequently. In some cases, it has been the sole intervention. The client is not instructed to do anything, certainly nothing specific. Whatever instructions are given are general and vague: "This week, it would be very important not to do anything to bring about further improvement." Most of the intervention consists in offering believable rationales for "going slow": that change, even for the better, requires adjusting to; or that one needs to determine, a step at a time, how much change would be optimal as opposed to maximal: "You might be better off with a 75 percent improvement rather than a 100 percent improvement"; or "Change occurring slowly and step by step makes for a more solid change than change which occurs too suddenly."

In the following example, a patient who is in the midst of selling his home has presented complaints of feeling depressed, losing a job, and having conflicts with his girl friend. He is told at the end of the first interview to "go slow."

Th: There is one other thing I want to pass on to you. I sense what you have been describing to us is that you have received a large number of blows. I realize that these are events that have taken place, but another way of looking at them is psychological blows, and they have been unexpected, rapid, and they have

come together. They took you by surprise. You've lost a job,
this relationship is up in the air, she moves away, there has been
a loss of friends, and this whole thing becomes very confusing.
You're not completing tasks, and your whole feeling about
yourself feels low, and we feel very strongly that you're underestimating the impact of what you've experienced. You're almost doing yourself a disservice because we're surprised that
you're not feeling a hell of a lot worse—that you're not a lot
more depressed than you are—considering all that has happened
to you. And, if anything, we're surprised how well you're doing.

Pt: There are times when I get a lot worse.

Th: That doesn't surprise us. It seems quite appropriate.

Pt: It's carrying on too long. I've got to take care of it. [Call
from observation room.]

Th: My colleagues really feel you're underestimating the situation, especially the idea of down time—the time needed to recover. And while it's very unpleasant, there is a certain timing
and pacing to things. Just as if you had been hit by a car, you
would need down time to recover, to mend. Additionally, some
of the blows you received were close to knockout blows, and
your resources are low right now, which translates into "I can't
organize myself, etc." Therefore, you need to take it real easy
and go real slow, and not try to solve everything right away.
Hold back, do very little this week. Make only the minimal
changes this week. You need time to recover.

   The injunction to go slow will often be given very early—
quite possibly in the first session—with clients whose main attempted solution is "trying too hard," or with clients who press
the therapist with urgent demands for remedial actions while
they remain passive or uncooperative. Also, with few exceptions, this tack should be taken where the client, after being
given a specific intervention, has returned to the next interview
reporting some definite and welcome improvement. In such a
circumstance, even if the injunction to go slow is not used specifically, we would avoid any indication of overt optimism and
further encouragement. Rather, we much prefer to acknowledge

the good news, but then assume a worried expression and explain that, welcome as the change may be, it is too fast—that
such rapid improvement makes the therapist uneasy. On that
basis, the patients are urged to hold back any further improvement at least until the next appointment. The therapist may
even suggest that the improvement was so fast that some exacerbation of the symptom is called for. In keeping with the go slow
strategy, the next appointment is usually set for two weeks rather than for the following week. This is both consistent with
the idea of going slow and also an implicit reward, since the patient is required to spend less time and/or money on treatment.
To illustrate, let us return to the example of the depressed patient from the previous example who returned a week later and
reported that he felt "less depressed" and had completed some
tasks:

Th: It's good to hear that you have done some things this
week and that you report that you feel less depressed, but our
basic feeling is that you're moving too fast, and the important
thing is you need to slow down, and this is the big trap for
someone with your kind of problem—it's going too fast. It's
understandable that you want to come out of it right away, as
soon as possible; you don't feel good, but that's the pitfall—the
quicksand—and there are a number of points about slowing
down. For one thing, you are still depressed, you're not out of
it, and one of the traps for you is thinking you're out of the
woods, prematurely. As we said last week, there are a number
of things that have happened to you, and you need some down
time to recover. So you need to go slow. Secondly, the issues
you're dealing with now—job, relationships, moving—are complex and they're confused for you right now. And there is a real
pitfall in taking action until these things are clarified. Yet the
tendency is to want to do something. Third, a number of my
colleagues feel that your style is analytical and thinking things
out clearly, before making a move. And this is a time when you
can trip yourself up. When things are unclear, one must wait for
them to get clearer before taking action. Now this is difficult
to do, and there is "You want to do something." If you are

tempted to take action, one of my colleagues suggested that the action should be totally irrelevant to the problems you're facing.

Pt: OK, but one of the things I'm involved in now is this house. I have to spend time and attention on the closing of this house, which is probably about the twentieth of October.

Th: Well, our Associate Director was the one who just buzzed in. He said if there are things that you just have to do, you'll have to do them, but do them to the absolute minimum. I think you can condense everything I've said into one major theme: Your prime directive is that you need to go slow and hold off on any major action. And to keep with that, I would like to meet with you in two weeks instead of one to help slow things down.

This tactic, we believe, is useful because it portrays the therapist as uncommitted to changing the patient, certainly quickly, and therefore induces implicit pressure on the patient to cooperate with any suggestions or advice the therapist may subsequently give. At the same time, it removes a sense of urgency for the patient—an urgency that probably has been fueling his persistent attempts at "solving" his problem. That is, the client has been trying too hard to solve his problem and he is more likely to relax his problem-maintaining efforts if he is told that a satisfactory resolution of the problem depends on his proceeding slowly.

2. The Dangers of Improvement

In some ways, this can be viewed as an extension or variant of the "go slow" intervention. We are treating it separately since it can have somewhat different purposes and is often applied to certain kinds of patient resistance.

Here, the patient is asked if he can recognize the dangers inherent in resolving his problem. (He is not asked *if* there would be any dangers.) Most of the time, the patient will quickly reply that there could not be any dangers, that the resolution of the problem would simply make him happier, and so on. Without too much need for imagination, however, the therapist

to the wisdom, concern, thoughtfulness, and brilliance of the therapist: "You've helped me so much, I really can't thank you enough" or variations on such expressions of gratitude. Such adulation, however pleasing to receive, puts the therapist in a one-up position, and this can be a disadvantage to the client on terminating. It implicitly disqualifies the client's own accomplishments in the course of treatment and thereby defines him as less in control of the events of his life and more vulnerable to other, unforeseen, problems. This is a view conducive to problem formation. While the therapist cannot stop patients from expressing their gratitude, nor is there any need to, he can, nevertheless, reframe the accomplishments of treatment so that he is not in a one-up position. Perhaps the simplest way to accomplish that is by acknowledging the gratitude but indicating the client's own contribution to the success of the treatment—the information he was willing to give the therapist and its clarity, his willingness to try out tasks and to adopt new ways of dealing with events, his allowing other family members to be participants in therapy, and so forth. At the same time, the therapist can downgrade his own contribution: "It's not brilliance but just that I'm in the advantageous spot of being outside the forest. That's all."

Terminating When the Complaint Is Not Resolved

When a problem has not been resolved, treatment may terminate in two principal ways: In time-limited treatment, where there is a maximum number of sessions (most often ranging from six to twenty), therapy will terminate when the agreed-on sessions have been spent, even though the problem is unresolved. More often, treatment is open-ended, and here the client will usually initiate termination when the problem is unresolved. Because time-limited therapy is less frequent, we will first deal briefly with those terminations. In some cases, a time limit on treatment can enhance resolution of the problem because there is implicit pressure on the client to cooperate with the therapist (and on the therapist to get down to business). However, in a number of cases, the time limit can also pose an obstacle because the therapist may not have time to regear his strategy if he finds that his original thrust is not working. A therapist may find the last session arriving without any clear indication the problem has been resolved. She will then have to make a choice: She can attempt to use that session as a last-ditch effort to resolve the problem, or she can attempt to find out why her strategy failed. We believe there is less error in taking the latter course—for two main reasons. First of all, if the therapist's strategy has failed to resolve the problem, it is highly unlikely that persisting with that strategy will achieve results at the eleventh hour. Second, most interventions require some action by the client, which the therapist needs to check on in a subsequent session: Has the patient carried out the suggestion, in what way, and with what result? If a new kind of intervention is attempted in a last session, there is no opportunity to carry out this basic checkup. Finally, when things have not gone well for a strategically oriented therapist, it is more likely that the therapist has been working too hard rather than not hard enough.

Usually it is best to start the final appointment with the opener "As you know, this is our last session. As far as I can tell, nothing has really changed in your problem, and I don't think I've been of any help." Sometimes, when put this flatly, the patient will try to reassure the therapist: "Oh, no, I wouldn't say that. It's really been quite helpful for me to come in and talk with you." Instead of supporting this idea, the therapist might respond that the patient is being generous and, in any event, she feels that she might have been of more help. This aids in shifting to the useful closing question: "What, in your best judgment, do you feel was done or not done that may have hindered your resolving your problem?"

In most instances, it is the client who will initiate or insist on termination if the problem has not been resolved. Whether it is done on the phone or face to face, the client will express dissatisfaction with treatment. Such an expression may be mildly put: "I don't think too much has been happening lately, and I think it might be best if I see how I do on my own right now. So, if it's all right with you, I would like to stop treatment at this point. If it doesn't work out, I would call you." Or it will be more bluntly stated: "I don't think anything has really happened, and it would be a waste of time to pursue things here further. So, I've come in this last time to tell you I want to stop treatment. Of course, if you see some reason why I should continue, I might consider it." In such cases, the therapist should avoid at all costs the temptation to challenge the client's position and to urge him to remain in treatment. The urging may not be explicit; rather, the therapist will question the client's decision or will suggest that the decision is based on some kind of resistance. It can be very difficult to avoid this temptation when the client is saying that nothing has happened and the therapist believes that identifiable improvements have taken place. The therapist is likely to try to point out those gains and will become increasingly frustrated as the client discounts them and sticks doggedly to the position that nothing has changed.

Instead of slipping into that counterproductive struggle, the therapist should readily accept the client's wish to terminate. At the very least, a gracious departure may allow the client easier reentry into treatment if he feels he needs it later on:

Pt: I really don't think we've gotten anywhere, and I'm having just as much trouble as when I came in. So, if it's all right, I would like to make this my last session.

Th: Yes, I think that would be best. I can't see that anything has happened either, and I too get frustrated when that continues. It's not the way I like to earn my fees.

On occasion, when the therapist takes a flexible stance, the client may soften his position by asking for some parting advice or suggestion from his therapist: "Even though this is my last session, I was wondering if you have any suggestions; is there anything I can do that might be of help?" As mentioned before, there is little point to a last-ditch effort in a final session. Even if the therapist can offer something new, the client is not likely to accept or act on that parting advice. It is more advantageous to maintain the gracious and "one-down" position started with: "Considering that I haven't done anything for you after all this time, I'm flattered you still have confidence in me to ask for advice. I'm sorry to have to disappoint you, though, because I don't have any brilliant ideas right now. Besides, I wouldn't trust any advice I gave you, since I'm likely just to repeat past errors." A similar position can be taken if the client asks for a referral: "I think it could be a good idea to get help from someone else, but I'd rather not suggest whom you might see, since my own biases might influence that. Since I haven't helped you, you really should make a fresh start with someone of your own choosing or, at least, referred by someone other than me."

The therapist might depart from a gracious, one-down position in cases where the client has been uncooperative during treatment, refusing or "forgetting" to act on suggestions and posing other obstructions. When the client expresses dissatisfaction with treatment and is suggesting termination, the therapist can readily agree, but with a different framing than that described. Instead, he can state that termination is desirable, not because of lack of progress but because of the risk that the problem might be resolved if treatment continued; that resolution might produce an unanticipated change—for example, in the client's marriage—that could be detrimental to the client. If needed, the therapist can support that opinion by citing previous instances of uncooperativeness, defining these as indicating the client's "unconscious wisdom" in avoiding change. While this framing may sound harsh, its purpose is to maximize any chance that, even though treatment is ending, the patient may yet come to terms with his problem. It can do this by putting the patient in the position of having to agree or disagree with the therapist's dour conclusion. If he agrees, he is redefining his complaint as "no problem" or, at least, not enough of a problem to warrant further treatment. In defining it that way, he will be less likely to struggle with his problem and may therefore find his problem lessening. If he disagrees with the therapist, he will have taken up an implicit challenge which requires that he resolve his problem. If he then continues treatment with someone else, he will be more likely to resolve his problem by not using that therapist as his foil in passive resistance to useful suggestions. Thus, there is more chance that he will depart from his previous position of "Cure me, I dare you" to one of actively utilizing treatment purposefully.

As a concrete example, we offer the closing dialogue with a patient who had failed to show any improvement in the ten sessions allocated in the Brief Therapy Center. His complaint was originally stated as "procrastinating at work." Throughout treatment, he had tenaciously attempted to engage the therapist in abstract discussions of his history and unconscious factors he proposed as significant for his problem. When it appeared that he would passively resist any tasks or assignments—usually through procrastination—the therapist shifted to a strategy of "Don't change." In the final minutes of the last session, the patient asks the therapist to comment on the possibility of further, insight-oriented treatment:

Th: While we have nine minutes left, I think this is an appropriate stopping point.

Pt: OK. The one question I had left is: What is the argument? Is there a strong argument to be made in favor of exploration?

Th: Well, I think all the arguments have been put. And mainly, it's my colleagues' thought that the strong argument is that, as far as they're concerned, your problem should not be resolved. [Call from colleague in observation room.] Yeah, something I forgot is that, in a sense, you've got it made. Your boss has said, "Take all the time you want. Glad to hear you're getting professional help." No salary increase, but no cut.

Pt: That's not the argument. He expects, and I think deserves, that . . . you know, potential improvement. [Call from observation room.] Yeah, I guess it's time to go. [Laughs.]

Th: Well, what's the difference between saying to somebody "I'd like you to do this" or saying to somebody "I'd like you to try"? They would like to see it, but they don't fully expect it to come about. And that's the difference of that wording. Anyhow, lots of luck.

Finally, on occasion there are patients who ask to terminate treatment when the problem has not been resolved but who, surprisingly, indicate satisfaction with the outcome: "Things have been a little bit better for a while now, and I was wondering if I might taper off treatment or maybe even stop. There are some things coming up I need to take care of, and time is going to be tight for me." There is no way of knowing whether the patient is dissatisfied with treatment and is just begging off politely or whether the patient is sufficiently satisfied with the outcome, modest as that outcome may seem. In either case, there is little point in challenging his wish to stop. If the patient is dissatisfied with treatment, the therapist will only get into a futile struggle; and if the patient is satisfied with the outcome, the therapist will be trying to get him to prolong a treatment he is already feeling he has concluded. In the final analysis, since significant dissatisfaction with one's life leads one into treatment, the cessation of that level of dissatisfaction is the general and ultimate goal—as we see it—in all cases.

❧ 9 ❧

Case Study

The Aversive
Adolescent

Having described and briefly illustrated the basic features of our approach, we will now—in this chapter and the two that follow it—present more extensive case material to provide a synthesis that shows how these various elements come together in actual practice. Each chapter consists of verbatim transcriptions from tape recordings of therapist-patient dialogue. Interspersed among these transcriptions are explanatory notes, consisting primarily of retrospective comments on the information provided by the clients and on the strategic rationale behind the therapist's statements, questions, and directives. Treatment in the first and third cases involved five interviews, each interview approximately one hour in length. Given this volume of material, which could easily fill a book of its own, we have chosen to present excerpts from

189

each interview, to give the reader a succinct but comprehensive overview of the treatment. The second case, The Anxious Violinist, involved only one complete interview and a brief follow-up interview. This material is presented almost in its entirety. The three cases taken together—one a teenage problem, one an adult problem, one a problem of later life—provide an illustration of our work with a range of problems.

In the following case, the parents of a fifteen-year-old girl had contacted the Brief Therapy Center at the suggestion of their daughter's probation officer. She had run away from home, and had been temporarily placed in the Juvenile Hall, but was now home again. The parents are in their early forties and the daughter, Suzie, is the oldest of four children. As is common in our way of working, the parents were asked to come in without their daughter for that first session. In addition to the fifteen-year-old, they have three younger children (twelve, ten, and eight years of age), who were never seen. Paul Watzlawick was the primary therapist in this case.

Session 1

Excerpt 1

Th: Would you—even though I know it's about your daughter and her trouble with the law—would you tell me what brings you here?

F: Well, we both feel, and I think even *she* feels, that she does things and she doesn't even know why she does them. You know? Like, she's always saying . . . Well, a few instances. She thinks that everyone is against her. She's always saying, "Everybody in this family is against me. Everybody hates me," and all this type of stuff, and we can't see that we do, you know. We feel like we treat all the kids the same. And she's kind of got a complex about being persecuted, and it don't seem that way to us, you know. And everything she does—she just revolts against everything.

M: Constant fighting. Constant, never-ending fighting.

F: Argues about every little thing that comes along. She'll start a fight over it. And she fights with the other kids and fights with my wife. Argues about everything. And she's just been in one trouble after another.

M: She never gets in any, you know, *big* trouble.

F: Like even this thing with the law. The reason she was down at Juvenile Hall was she ran away. She didn't commit a crime other than running away, and this is the second time she's done this. Once before, she ran away, last summer. And she went over to the beach, and I found out where she was at, and I went over there. And this guy came over, a friend of hers, and another thing about her: It seems like she just . . . Every time some guy comes around, she's right with the guy, you know? Like she's almost man crazy.

In this short interchange, the parents give a rather clear picture of the problem, primarily involving their daughter's abrasive behavior in the family and her running away. While they begin by referring to her not knowing why she does things and by the comment "And she's got a complex about being persecuted," statements which would indicate a view she is "sick," they subsequently clarify their position as one of viewing her behavior as "bad": "She just revolts against everything," "Constant fighting. Constant, never-ending fighting," "argues about every little thing," "been in one trouble after another."

Excerpt 2

F: So this friend of mine lives in a town in Wyoming, and he's a minister, and he talked it over with his wife, and he has four children of his own. And he works real good with kids. I mean, he gets along real good with kids, and we thought, well, maybe that'd be . . . we'll let her go to school there for a year. Her parents live there; my parents live there—my mother does—and we got a lot of relatives there. And we thought, well, maybe that'd be good. So we went up there on vacation in August, and then she stayed there and went to school for two months. Well, I went up in October and brought her back 'cause she was acting up up there the same way she was doing here. You know, she went out one night and got drunk, and raised all kinds of heck and everything.

Excerpt 3

F: Then I just took off, and I called the police and went over there and picked her up, and she·just came to the door. I said, "Is Suzie there?" And one of these guys said, "Yeah, she's here, she's in watching TV." And he says, "Suzie, your dad wants you." So she came to the door and she says, "I'm not going home. I hate it at home." And I said, "Well, I never said you were going home." I said, "You're going for a ride with this policeman." And she said, "Where to?" And I said, "Well where he usually takes kids like you, down to Juvenile Hall." "I'm not going down there," and she started arguing and yelling. And then finally she just got in the car and she got ready, and she was going to go. But she went down to . . . The police officer brought me back home. So she got out of the car and she said, "Could I talk to you for just a minute?" And I said, "Yeah." And she got out of the car and she says, "I don't know why . . . I didn't do this to hurt you." And I said, "What do you mean you didn't do this to hurt me?" I said, "You've been trusted so many times, and every time you break the trust and do what you want to do." She says, "I just hate everybody else; I don't hate you too bad, but I hate Mom. I don't know why you just don't divorce her, and I could live with you." And I said, "Oh, that would really be nice, Suzie," and so I said, "Well, good-bye," and I put her in the police car and she went down to Juvenile Hall.

The father is indicating some of the things they have done to try to deal with Suzie's misbehavior: turning to "experts": first to their minister friend ("who works real good with kids" and would also provide a change of scene) and then to the authorities. This segment also illustrates another point in doing therapy briefly, knowing what not to bother with. The daughter is indicating an alliance with the father against the mother: "I don't know why you just don't divorce her, and I could live with you." The mentioning of such a suggested coalition could tempt a therapist to probe further for presumed marital pathology. However, since the father responded to her by summarily dismissing her proposal and by persisting with his plan to allow the police to handle her runaway, the therapist did not pursue this avenue of investigation.

Excerpt 4

F: And another thing, I think she grew up too fast. She's developed like a gal twenty-five years old. I mean she's about 5'7", weighs 130 pounds, got a 40" bust line, and I mean all these kids running around with her are little kids, and she's been that way for about two years, I'd say. Since she was about thirteen years old.

M: She *thinks* that she's this old. I mean, she feels, if you talk to her, that she is capable of making major decisions and handling any kind of problem that comes up, and so . . . When she does ask you something—she asks—she spends her life asking, you know, "Can I this? Can I that?" and it's true—half the things, it's "No." That's what I said to him last night: It seems like we say so many "No's" to Suzie, but she asks 30,000 things a day, you know, where the other kids, it just seems like they ask a couple things. She comes in, and she gets up in the morning with "Can I?" She's already, sometimes, planning, you know, what she's gonna do at 7:00 tonight. Or at breakfast she's worried about what we'll have for dinner tomorrow night. Things like this. So it is a never-ending—it seems like—a thing of "No."

F: It seems to me she has nothing to do at all with our family. She comes home. She'll come in at dinner time, she'll sit down, and she'll just, as soon as the dinner's on the table, she'll just take a fork and just . . . She's so, just wound up with nervousness.

M: She's extremely nervous.

F: And her foot just—she just taps her foot while she eats. And she just eats so fast that you can't believe it. I mean, everybody else is just getting started, and she says, "I'm gonna watch television." She gets up and walks in the front room.

M: And you say, "Oh no, you're not. Now you just sit down
and eat with the rest of us." It's at this point—and it has been
for a while—that she's mad.

The parents elaborate on the problems they face with
Suzie and, at the same time, confirm their position of "she's
bad." Even where they describe her "nervousness," they define
it as impatience and are willing to insist she take her time eating
and not rush away from the table to watch the TV.

Excerpt 5
M: "I hear you cut class." "How do you know?" I said, "The
school called." So she said, "No, I didn't." I said, "Yes, you
did." I said, "They called me and asked me if you were sick
Thursday." "All right, I did." And I said, "All right, Suzie, now
I'd like to know where you were from noon until 6:30." "Nowhere." I says, "Where were you?" So we go this route. She
says, "I was nowhere." I said, "I want to know where you were,
whom you were with, and what you were doing." She says,
"I was nowhere, with nobody, doing nothing." So, I said, "Well,
all right. Then I hate to tell your dad this; that's all I get
done is run and tattle on you. Then he's upset, then everything
flares up." She said, "Go ahead and tell him. He'll ground me.
Big deal, ground me." And I said, "Even if I don't tell him,
Suzie," I said, "I'm grounding you. And I could tell you that
right now because . . ."

This is a fine example of "doing more of the same"; that
is, sticking with a "solution" even though it is not working. The
mother interrogates Suzie, gets an unsatisfactory response, but
continues to interrogate even though she only gets more of the
same responses. Also, she attempts to intimidate Suzie by telling her that her father will "ground" her. When this does not intimidate her, she says, ineffectually, "I'm grounding you." This
segment also exemplifies part of their attempted solution—to
confront Suzie and ask for a self-indictment, trying to wrest an
admission that she was in the wrong.

Excerpt 6

F: Well, like Thanksgiving Day. She's there. And we had the dinner, and we had relatives come, and her brother and his family was coming over, and everyone was coming over. So Suzie said, "I need a pair of nylons. I don't have any nylons. I want to dress up today." And Martha [the mother] said to her, "Look, why do you need to dress up? All the girls are coming over, and you'll all be outside and everything. Why don't you just wear a pair of jeans or a pair of pants or something?" "I don't feel like it. Today's a holiday, and at least I could have a pair of nylons. I don't have any." And everything. So finally I give her the money, and she went out and bought nylons. So the same day she wrecked the nylons. Then two days later she called me and said, "Can I get a pair of nylons for school?" I said, "I just bought you a pair the other day." I said, "I can't buy you a pair of nylons every day." "Well, I don't know why I can't have a pair. I need them for school, you know. I can't wear a dress without having nylons. I gotta have them to wear to school." And I said, "OK." Now, if I would have said, "No, that's it. You're not getting a pair till next week." "Oh, God," she'd have slammed the phone down. You know, she just can't take no. I mean, you've just got to do it her way or else there's a civil war.

Excerpt 7

M: We've often said she has a knack for breaking anybody down—people that know her will tell you this, even kids—with her persistence. And she got into such a—she mastered this. I look back, and I can remember a thousand times saying, "Yes, you can. Just leave me alone." I'd say, "No, Suzie," first of all, and I'd sometimes—I mean, a lot of times, I'll admit I say "No" because every day it's a thousand things.

Excerpt 8

Th: Since she has a way—apparently, a very, very powerful technique—of breaking you down—both of you, apparently—and obviously this is not a reasonable thing. This is a thing that just grates on your nerves. It isn't . . . she doesn't break you down with reason; she breaks you down with unreason.

At this point, the therapist decides to intervene. This is relatively fast, coming as it does in the first half of the very first session. However, there are a number of reasons why he can intervene so rapidly: The parents have, on minimal inquiry, given a succinct but clear picture of the problem and the ways that they have attempted to deal with it. Part of that clarity comes from the simplicity of their language, their use of verbatim reports, examples, and simulations of Suzie's tone of voice (which, of course, cannot be conveyed in a written transcript). Second, they are clearly defining her behavior as "bad," and they are therefore not likely to be concerned about "damaging her psyche" should they be asked to institute measures that are required for parental control but that might disadvantage Suzie.

The therapist begins his intervention by paraphrasing their own complaints and using some of their own vocabulary, such as "breaking you down." Starting this way establishes a therapist's credibility. Then he continues by beginning to reframe the problem. He has been noting that a central factor in their attempted solution is confronting Suzie and trying to get her to be compliant through harangue and exhortation. His reframing, then, begins by labeling what she does as "unreason" instead of "rebellion."

M: Persistence, right.

Th: Persistence. I'm wondering, you know, what could the two of you do that would be along the same lines? You know, give her some of her own medicine, so to speak. Obviously, she has a breaking point; one can grate on her nerves just as she can grate on yours. And, give me some idea—can you help me there?

F: Well, I think the thing is, what we've done this last week. Just tell her "No."

   Excerpt 9
F: She said, "What do you mean?" She said, "I can't go out

after dinner; now I can't even go out before dinner. Why don't I just go to prison?"

M: "My day's wrecked."

F: "My day is wrecked," and everything, and started yelling. And I said, "I don't want to discuss it any further. Stay home." And I hung the phone up.

Th: And what did she do?

F: She stayed home.

It appears that when the father has said "No" without getting entangled in "reasoning" with the daughter, Suzie has complied.

Excerpt 10

Th: Suppose for a moment that the two of you could envision the possibility of giving her some of her own medicine.

M: I'd like to; I don't know what it is.

Th: Trying to counter her with reason doesn't seem to get you very far, it sounds at least.

M: It doesn't.

F: This past week, this is what we've tried to do.

Th: All right, but, yeah, the past week you've tried to be strict in a consistent way.

M: But me, though, I've been staying out of the picture.

Th: But in a sense, you are still being reasonable. And I'm just wondering, you know, for the purpose of this exploration of this preliminary talk with you . . . I'm just wondering, could you think of a way in which the two of you, yourselves, could be unreasonable? And make things very, very difficult for her, just as she makes things difficult for you because all she has to do is to be unreasonable. And then you try to reason, and nothing comes of it.

M: I'd like to know something because I'd like to . . .

Th: Well, you must have thought of something.

Once having reframed the problem as Suzie's "unreasonableness," and an "unreasonableness" that constantly frustrates their efforts, the therapist builds on that to a next step. He is now asking them what they might do that could match her power of unreasonableness. Since they are groping and uncertain, he makes the task more pointed: "But in a sense, you are still being reasonable. Can you think of a way of being unreasonable?" In addressing themselves to this task, they are accepting that being "unreasonable" will be a more effective method than their former approach of direct confrontation. The parents are giving the therapist clear "yes" responses—go-ahead signals—in this passage.

F: You know, you could just say to her, instead of like when she says, "Could I have that purse?" Just say, "No." You know . . . you see, she walks to the next thing and she says, "Can I have this?" And I say, "Suzie, what do you want to buy that for?" And I try to explain to her. I think if you just got like she is. Like she says something, and you say, "Suzie, why? Can't you do this or that?" "I don't know." I mean, if you just got like her, and when she comes home and says, "Can I go up to Carol's," just say, "No." And if she says, "Why not?" instead of saying, "Oh, you've got homework, and you've got to clean your room," just say, "That's it. 'Cause I *said* no."

Th: Or you could say, "Because this is Friday." Or something like that. [The day was Wednesday.]

F: Yeah, just give her some of the ridiculous answers she gives us.

Th: Yeah.

The father has finally "gotten the message" and offers an adequate example of how they might now be less "reasonable" and more arbitrary. The therapist supports this effort by accepting it and offering a variant on it, a way of implying "All right, you're on the right path now." In turn, the father confirms his grasp of the anticipated shift in their dealings with Suzie: "Yeah, just give her some of the ridiculous answers she gives us." It is uncertain how much the mother is accepting this new tack, but the therapist prefers to settle for a small gain and does not try to further engage the mother in the maneuver.

Excerpt 11
Th: I don't want you to do anything differently from what you've been doing, but I do wonder if, perhaps, until next Wednesday, you could, at least in your minds, imagine how in a given situation you could deal with her differently. And, by differently, I mean mostly unreasonably. Don't do it. But try to—in the thick of the battle—try to think how you could do it differently. Without doing it. Just exercise it, or rehearse it through in your mind.

While the therapist's closing instruction would seem to put some restraint on implementing the new approach, it actually enhances its being put into practice. By appearing to hold it back, he is avoiding the risk of their rejecting the idea after the session, a risk which would be greater if they felt under some pressure to carry it out. Second, he is telling them to *think* about how they might implement it and to do that thinking under circumstances where they would be most tempted to try it out, when Suzie is being provocative.

Session 2

Suzie has been brought in at the therapist's request, and the first part of this session is with father, mother, and daughter present.

Excerpt 12
Th: [Addressing Suzie] And what would you like to see changed in your family? So, even if you were to think of it only in very selfish terms, you know, not taking into account what might be good for everybody, or might be preferable for everybody. But if you were to think of it strictly in terms of your own advantage, what would you like to see changed in the family?
D: If there wasn't any fighting.

Th: If there wasn't any fighting, OK. Could you be a bit more specific?

D: That's it. That's all we do is fight.

Since Suzie is not a willing participant in therapy, the therapist engages her participation by asking her what she, personally, would like to see changed in the family, instead of asking her "What is the problem?" Unexpectedly, she emphasizes fighting in the family.

Excerpt 13

Th: You have—I don't know how, over time—but it seems that you have gotten yourself into an extremely powerful position. Your parents, even though they are making noises—you know, that you are bad, and you should change, and this is unacceptable, and that is unacceptable—but on the whole, I think your parents sound pretty helpless. Now for two adults to be helpless, I think this is rather extraordinary. And, if anything, it shows that you are extremely good at making them helpless. The impression we got last time is that the best way for you to maintain the power that you have—apparently, over the entire family—the best way for you will be, whenever you ask for something and they say "No," it might be very useful if you were then to say "Why not?"

D: I say "Why not?"

Th: All right. I know that you do that. I just want to confirm something. By saying "Why not?" you are going to force them into having to give you their reasons.

D: They don't. They tell me—they just say, " 'Cause I said so."

Th: Well, you know, but I got the impression last time, apparently your mother sees it differently. Your father too. Apparently, they are rather eager to explain to you why not. And this is where your main trump card lies. If you can involve them into some kind of an argument—"Why not?"—and then if you persist long enough, your parents, but mostly your mother, is then likely to give up, in sheer desperation or exasperation, and say, "Do it. I'm fed up, I can't stand this anymore." So you have the power to drive them up the wall. They may say "No" at first, but so what? You've been through this. And you know how to deal with a "No." And I think you, strictly from your point of view, you would be stupid to give up that power. And if you insist long enough, you're getting what you want. Now there's a certain price to this. Nothing is, you know . . . Everything in this life costs something, and there's a price for that. And the price may be that you are in a chronic state of rage because you have to appear angry for all the things that are being done to you. And every once in awhile you may finish up in Juvenile Hall, which you're going to get used to. You know, it's just the first few times that it's unpleasant. But you can get used to that. And, who knows, if you can't develop methods to drive *them* up the wall too? So what now remains for me to do is to help your parents to learn this, to learn to put up with this. And for this I don't need you here. So would you mind waiting in the waiting room? [Suzie leaves; remainder of therapy is with parents only.]

The therapist temporarily moves from Suzie's complaint about "fighting" to her role in provoking the parents into their characteristic defensive posture of explaining and exhorting, illustrating this by offering examples of the likely dialogue which has gone on at home. However, he redefines that provocation as a special "ability" and one that puts her in a power position. He then urges her not to depart from this effective stance, and appears to brush aside the consequences she could face in trying to maintain her "powerful" position—though he mentions them, including more fighting. In doing all this, the therapist is facing Suzie with a "symptom prescription" to continue her difficult behavior; thus, he avoids enmeshment in an attempted solution that has failed: asking her to behave better. At the same time, for the parents' ears, he is redefining Suzie's abrasive behavior as not just spontaneous selfishness but a calculated effort to control them and "drive them up the wall." Finally, he summarily dismisses her from the session, a move that implicitly affirms his coalition with the parents.

Excerpt 14

Th: What, if anything, have the two of you been able to come up with in your own minds, just on a thinking level, by a way of a different way of dealing with this?

M: I don't know. I can't think of anything. I'm helpless.

F: I just say, when she wants to do something, just say "No" and don't explain nothing to her. Be like she is.

M: Oh yeah, what was it.

F: Like if she says "I want to do something," just say "No," and if she says "Why not?" just say "Because we're going to the beach next month." You know, just give her some ridiculous answer, just like . . .

The father indicates he has accepted the tack of "unreasonableness" and is able to carry it out. The mother, however, appears to be struggling with the concept and is at a loss to know what to do with it; she says she is "helpless."

Excerpt 15

Th: [Addressing mother] You have so far tried to either reason with her or, if the reasoning is unsuccessful, to show some strength. You yourself have admitted that showing strength is useless because she can—if the two of you were to come to blows—she's probably the stronger of the two. Now that's exactly not what we want you to do. What I would like you to do is to leave this interview pretending—and I use this word advisedly—pretending that I have made things very, very difficult for you. I have taken her side. I have blamed you for having been a bad mother, for having made all kinds of mistakes. And that this is the outcome; this is why there is now this unrest and this unhappiness in the family. So this gives you a convenient excuse to then do what I would like you to do. First you have to have an excuse why your behavior suddenly changes. And the excuse is that I have been very, very critical.

M: OK.

The therapist is satisfied with the father's response, and

he now turns to the mother. Instead of urging her to adopt the approach of "unreasonableness" that the father is ready to take, he redefines the problem somewhat differently for her, focusing on what he is calling her unsuccessful position of attempted "strength."

This shift in reframing for the mother is in keeping with the basic principle of using what the client brings rather than struggling to get the client to change a style or value. The mother, unlike her husband, is not as comfortable taking an openly arbitrary position. At the same time, she is acting befuddled and passive. The therapist has decided to use those qualities, since passive befuddlement can also be a way of avoiding a provocative confrontation with their daughter. Thus, he begins by suggesting that she depart from her position of "strength" and, instead, adopt one of apparent "weakness." The mother indicates that she is accepting this reframing.

Th: And then, because you are so upset and depressed, you do all kinds of stupid things, but only with her. Not with the others, not with you [the father]. But it so happens that whenever she asks you for something, the thing is either not at home, or you have broken it, or you have lost it. I cannot go into the details because we simply don't have the time, but there are, of course, a hundred things that she depends on you for getting. Let me use here a couple of examples that may not be pertinent at all because I don't know your daily lives at home—the little things that you know too well. I want you, for instance, when she's gobbling down her dinner to get out on a date—I want you to do something very silly and spill a glass of milk over her. And then be very apologetic. Now, this is a difficult part that you are probably going to blow. You don't do this in a punitive way; you don't imply, "Aha, it serves you right." You are very apologetic: "Suzie, I'm terribly sorry. Oh my God; what do we do now? I don't know what's the matter with me these days. I'm so upset, and I'm so depressed, I've been doing all kinds of stupid things, you wouldn't believe it." I would like you to continue to make whatever reasonable demands you can make of her: Do the dishes, be home at a certain time, keep your room clean. But I want you—every time you make this demand, make a demand of this kind—I want you to add, "But if you don't do it, I cannot force you." So what I'm asking of you is a very big thing; I am asking you to completely change your attitude from strength to weakness. To helplessness. I want you to pretend that you are very helpless, and because you are helpless, there are all kinds of things that suddenly don't work out, that suddenly don't function. You understand me? I want you to . . . Suppose that the problem comes up that she's out, she's going out, and—does she have a . . . What time do you want her back? If she goes out in the evening?

F: Well, since she got out of this Juvenile Hall thing, she doesn't go out at night except . . .

Th: At all?

F: . . . on weekends. And if she goes on weekends, she goes to the movie or someplace and she comes right home.

Th: Comes right home. All right, let's assume that she doesn't come right home. And right home, let's assume, is 11:00. OK?

F: OK.

Th: What time do the two of you go to bed?

F: Oh, she usually goes to bed early, and I stay up half the night. Yeah, I stay up till 12:00 or 1:00.

Th: OK. That particular Saturday, or whenever she goes out next, would you mind going to bed a little earlier yourself? So that the house is completely dark, and all doors and windows are locked. Can this be done, or does she have a key?

F: No, she doesn't have a key.

Th: All right. So, if the time comes—let's say it's 11:00—the time comes when she's supposed to be home, and she isn't home, you lock the doors and windows, and you go to bed. When she comes home, she has to ring the bell. Or knock. Now, I want the two of you to wait very long—several minutes. Then I want you to go out and ask, as if in a confused way, who it is. And she'll say, of course, "It's me." And you let her in, no matter what time it is. If it's 1:00, it doesn't matter. You let her in and *apologize* for having let her wait so long. Or you, whoever gets up. And you stumble back into bed without even asking "Where were you? Why are you so late? You know you are on probation." She's on probation, right?

F: Right.

Th: "And you're supposed to be home by 11:00" or whatever time it is. No. Don't do that. And on the following morning, not a word, unless she brings it up. And then you apologize again: "I'm sorry if I left you out in the cold, but there is something the matter with me. I do the silliest things these days. I'm very upset."

The therapist makes the approach more explicit and, noting further "yes responses" (nodding), further clarifies the potential use of this approach by giving an example involving both parents. What he has done is to induce them, especially the mother, to back away from their former position of futile and helpless confrontation and, instead, adopt a procedure we have labeled "benign sabotage." While the "sabotage" aspect of this maneuver can be helpful in giving parents some feeling of power and control, and in posing real consequences for misbehavior, they are probably not as important as the "one-down" position the parent takes. The avoidance of a "one-up" position eliminates the provocative and rebellion-inducing behavior the parents have unwittingly been employing.

Session 3

Excerpt 16

Th: So, will you bring me up to date, please?

M: Well, we've just had all kinds of excitement—just doing what you said, you know. I've had Suzie in tears all week—total frustration, you know. An example is a couple days ago, where she said to me, "Is a sweater enough to wear to school today?" So I said, "Well, it's awfully cold, Suzie. A coat might be better." And she said, "But it might get hot this afternoon; then I'd have to carry it home." So I said, "Then probably a sweater would be fine." So she said, "You make me sick." She says, "I'm never speaking to you again," and left.

Th: Which means what to you?

M: I don't know, it just means I won't argue with her about anything, and that makes her mad.

F: She [mother] used to say, "You wear the coat to school. It's freezing cold, and if it gets warm, you carry it home and that's it." "Well, I don't know why I have to carry it if I don't want to. I'm the one that's gonna get cold," and she'd argue about it. But now, when she says something, I'll say, "Well, I'll think about it, Suzie. I'll see." And stuff like that.

M: Well, like the sewing machine, for instance.

F: She just goes—she just, like, she don't know what to say next 'cause no one will fight with her. You know, she tries all kinds of maneuvers to get into arguments. And when no one will argue with her, she just gets frustrated and don't know what to do, you know.

The therapist wants first to find out what the parents have done with the suggested tasks. They report that they were able to avoid their usual "reasonable" confrontations with Suzie and, instead, take a more quixotic stance. While they say that this seems to leave Suzie angrily frustrated, they are not bothered by that. (Their tone of voice more clearly indicates that not only are they not bothered by her frustration but are feeling they are beginning to get on top of the situation with her.)

Th: So, in this past week, you have tried—you made a good job out of not giving Suzie information. It would be much more powerful, of course, if you were unable to give information simply because you are so depressed and upset. She wants an answer. And this past week, you have said—most of the time—you have said, "I'll think it over." But I guess in saying "I'll think it over," you still exuded some kind of strength. "I'll let *you* know in my own good time. And in the meantime you will have to wait." This sounds still very much in a one-up . . . you know, one-up position—a position of strength. I would like you to take

father, the therapist is using that position as an extra entice-
ment to the patient. Essentially, the implicit message is "By
overcoming your problem, you can one-up your father."

Pt: Well, it's one, of course, I—a punch I would like to deliver.

Th: [Pause] Um. Well, maybe.

Pt: Oh, but I would, I . . . oh, yes.

Th: [Sighing] Well, OK. [Pause] No way I can—no way I can
dispute you except that I don't know, might shake you up more
than you would think to shake your old man up.

Pt: Well, I've shaken him up in the past through a few failures,
and through a few positive things . . .

Th: [Interrupting] You—with your old man, a failure wouldn't
shake him up nearly as bad as a success would [small laugh].

The patient has risen to the offer. The therapist, however,
does not encourage him but converts the offer into a challenge.
This tends to intensify the patient's motivation, since he now
has to prove to the therapist that he meant what he said, and he
can do so only by resolving the problem.

Pt: [Pause] True. But I wouldn't—I wouldn't mind just seeing
him being shaken up.

Th: OK. [Pause] Whose observation of your playing . . . well,
let me back off from that to ask a preliminary first. Is it just observation you're concerned about, or do you get actual criticism
when you do badly?

Pt: Is it just observation that I'm concerned about, or actual
criticism?

Th: Yeah. In other words, I'm wondering is there somebody
that is laying some words on you about "My God, you're flop-
ping there, and you oughta be able to get on with it," or is it
more you know people observe when you do poorly, and you
get shaky, but they're not talking about it?

Pt: Well, that's—this—that's it, more or less, the second time.

Th: OK. Whose observation would you be most concerned about?

Pt: [Sigh] Other violin teachers.

Th: Uh-huh.

Pt: Other knowledgeable violin teachers. There are several in this city that I would—I would be delighted to be able to perform well in front of.

Th: Uh-huh. [Pause] Do you know how to perform badly?

Pt: Uh, we tried that, and I was so nervous at the time that I wasn't—I could not make up my mind whether I should try to perform badly or not. Because I was unaware of the discussion that had taken place with my therapist.

Th: OK. I understood that—I may be wrong—but I understood from him a little bit different—that he had asked you to perform in a mediocre way.

Pt: Uh-huh.

Th: I'm saying something a little different. I'm saying, do you know how to perform really badly?

At this point, the therapist is probing for a different intervention, one of suggesting that the patient might make a deliberate effort to play badly. This tactical thrust is still in keeping with his overall strategy, that of having the patient depart from his attempted solution of trying harder to play well.

Pt: No. Probably not. I certainly can perform really badly, I assume, but I'm not . . .

Th: Oh, that's an assumption.

Pt: Well, I have never tried to perform badly.

Th: Uh-huh.

Pt: Nor even mediocrely.

Th: [Pause] Well, I think you might learn something by—if you're up to making the attempt to perform actually badly, but . . . I . . . I'm hesitant to say much more about that because that might be moving too fast. I don't think you've really thought enough yet about the possible consequences of getting over this problem. And by "getting over the problem," I mean at most getting over the really out of control anxiety. I certainly don't mean getting over all the anxieties we were talking about a few minutes ago. And it's hard to distinguish where is that line between the real shakes and the sort of anxiety that is natural, normal, and, up to a point, even useful when one is performing. To go back to my analogy, I don't mean that violin playing is at the level, of course, of athletic performance; but, as the athletes who have dealt with this problem will point out, you've got to get a little bit anxious to get up to do what you can, and maybe something comparable to that—that some degree of anxiety is a thing that you can turn to use when you get out there ready to go. But the main thing I'm saying is—I sure as hell would be reluctant to see you learn how to get more control of your anxiety, which you might do by learning how to play badly to start with, deliberately, until you'd looked at the potential consequences a good deal more, because if you start to move in this thing, it's—it's a snowball. Snowball in the sense that an improvement leads to more improvement. It's also a snowball in a more profound sense. As you do better, your horizons as to what you might do will widen. That both has the disadvantage that the severity of pressure of observation will increase, and whether—how the two would keep pace is very hard to judge. It also has the disadvantage that widening of horizons means a lot of choices will enter into your life that aren't there now; and, therefore, decisions will have to be made all over the place.

The therapist had decided not to pursue this tactic further, at least explicitly. He does not drop it but rather "shelves" it, leaving it as an implicit invitation that the patient may take up on his own. The therapist enhances that invitation by explaining that he is "shelving" it because it might be so effective that it would bring about improvement before the patient has had a chance to think over all the disadvantages of improving. (There are times when the therapist may opt to make implicit suggestions rather than explicit assignments. There is no hard and fast rule about this. Partly it depends on timing. For example, in this interview, the therapist has already started on a tactical path—the disadvantages of improvement—and it might dilute that thrust if he were to introduce an additional assignment. Partly it depends on the patient, whether he is an individual who is willing to accept explicit suggestions or whether he would balk at being told what to do.) The therapist ultimately decides to elaborate on his original tactic by offering another disadvantage of improvement, and he also speaks further about the normality, and even the positive value, of nervousness.

Pt: That's what you have agents for. When they're that wide.

Th: Well, OK, but either they gotta bring some decisions back to you, or at least you've got to make the decision "Who do I want to be my agent, and is he doing a good job?" And it gets, you know—as things expand, there just gets to be a lot larger and tougher decisions to make, and . . . We're going to have to stop shortly. Let me raise a couple of points with you while we're still here. First of all, what would be a significant but minimal improvement for you? And I mean—let me define that a little more. What, if it were to happen, would lead you to say, "Look, I'm not out of the woods, but I've made a definite first step."

Pt: [Pause] Uh . . .

The therapist has now shifted to a different agenda, that of asking the patient about treatment goals. He already has obtained sufficient data on the problem and how the patient and others have attempted to deal with it. Because this was a demonstration interview and the problem was a discrete one, he has already made a number of interventions but now is getting back to the data collection characteristic of an initial interview. The final item in that agenda is the patient's stated goals.

Th: And think it over, because this can be a very difficult thing to judge, and particularly to get some index that you can't just kid yourself about, you know.

Pt: Well, I've thought about that. It's possible a first step would not necessarily be a successful performance. A first step would be perhaps that someone was interested, other than myself, in it being a successful performance. That I had help on the problem. That I had knowledgeable help on the problem.

The patient's response to that question indicates that he is confusing means with ends. The therapist has asked him what he would like to achieve in therapy, at least as a minimal goal. The patient, however, is talking about what it would take to overcome the problem. Some obvious confusion follows, and in the ensuing interchanges the therapist attempts to have the patient clarify his goal.

Th: Uh, could you say a little more on that? I'm not sure I'm following you.

Pt: I said that a first step, or certainly a minimal cure, which I think would be reflected in the performance, would be my feeling that I was not alone.

Th: Oh. OK.

Pt: But at some point—I felt it would be important to someone besides myself that this piece sound better than I normally play it, under nervous conditions. And—some—that a person would have to be interested in me and—I'm saying—or these people would be interested in me. That would perhaps be something. And that they would be able to judge what was going on.

Th: [Pause] All right. Uh, suppose that were to be your mother. Would that fill the bill?

Pt: It could never—that's impractical. It could—would never be she.

Th: Well, OK, but since we're hypothetical anyway, uh . . .

Pt: Oh. Yes—yes, that would be reasonable.

Th: Uh-huh. [Pause] Why do you say that that could never be, coming back to the more practical level?

Pt: Elton John and Bach are exactly the same to her.

Th: [Pause] Well, OK, but I'm not quite sure how that fits because while she might not make a discrimination between one or the other, she might still be concerned that whatever you play you did it better.

Pt: But she is not a judge of it.

Th: OK, you mean . . .

Pt: [Interrupting] She does not—she . . .

Th: . . . her opinion—her opinion isn't worth a damn on it, anyway?

Pt: No. Not a damn.

Th: Uh-huh. So it has to be someone both concerned and knowledgeable?

Pt: Hopefully it is.

Th: Well then, according to—I'm trying to see if I got your definition . . .

Pt: [Interrupting] All right. Well, I mean knowledgeable of not only the music but of my particular problem and of some way of—of alleviating it.

Th: Uh-huh.

Pt: That's a person or persons that—have several requirements that are tricky to meet, and one of them is to be concerned about me, which, needless to say, is tricky, and knowledgeable—tricky . . .

Th: I could see a . . . a potential difficulty with that standard. Just suppose, for example, that the age of miracles is not past, and in some senses it isn't, because one of the funniest things about problems is that not always, but often, they come mysteriously and they go mysteriously. If yours was to go mysteriously, and you turned out to be really a good violinist—you might give a performance that went very well, and was well received, but it still wouldn't meet this specification because the people would be knowledgeable, they would be listening to you, they would appreciate your performance, but they wouldn't appreciate it in the sense that you were describing, because they might never know that you'd had the problem. There might be no sign of it. And they would just be appreciating how well you would be playing, and they wouldn't know what you had accomplished in terms of the problem to get there.

In the course of clarifying the patient's goal, the therapist quickly interjects another intervention—the apparently casual suggestion that his problem might disappear as mysteriously as it arose. Again, this intervention is still in keeping with the overall strategy, since the idea that the problem can disappear on its own may aid in interdicting the patient's "solution" of working so hard to overcome the problem. The therapist does not dwell on this intervention but keeps it on an implicit level by then asking how the knowledgeable audience would know that such a miracle had occurred.

Pt: That might be true. I don't think that would be the worst thing that could ever happen to me.

Th: [Receives instructions from earpiece.] Ah. My colleague has got a solution for that.

Pt: I will let him in [laughs].

Th: When you are in that position, at the start of your concert, you can get up and announce to the audience what your problem has been, and then you could play.

Here, the therapist has "seeded" another intervention. Because the time planned for the interview is almost over, he is not going to be able to develop that tactic, but still prefers to introduce it as an idea that the patient might take up on his own or that might be reintroduced by his regular therapist in a subsequent session if it seems appropriate. The intervention itself is based on the idea that if one doesn't attempt to conceal one's nervousness, one is likely to be more relaxed in performing, since expectations have been reduced—both one's own and the audience's.

Pt: I thought about that.

Th: Good. Uh, all right, is there anything on the matter of what would be a sign of a first step? Can you think of anything that would be a sort of visible sign? Or an audible sign? What, if it were to observably happen, would be an index or criterion that a first step—significant, although maybe small—has occurred?

The therapist now refines his question on goals, emphasizing that he is asking for visible or tangible measures. He has realized that the patient's initial responses indicated confusion between identifiable goals and the means required to achieve them or associated feelings.

Pt: That I got through an entire piece in a performance situation without a memory slip of any kind.

Th: [Pause] OK. That makes the first step pretty nearly the same as the final step.

Pt: Oh, no, no, no . . .

Th: No?

Pt: . . . no, no, no.

Th: What would be the final step?

Pt: The final step is to get through it without any memory slip *well.*

Th: Oh. OK. Let me see if I got the difference. If you got through it without any memory slip, but not necessarily well, that would be the first step?

Pt: Hmm-huh.

Th: Uh-huh.

Pt: "Well" is a big, big field.

Th: It's too bad you can't have a different sort of memory slip.

Pt: [Pause] How so?

Th: Well, all—all you'd have to do is, instead of forgetting the music, would be to forget the audience.

Here again, the therapist makes a "probing" intervention. He does not dwell on the point but has intimated that, by virtue of his problem of "memory slip," the patient can use that same mechanism to overcome his anxiety about the audience. In a sense, we would regard this intervention as a nontrance "hypnotic" suggestion. At the very least, it also implicitly redefines the problem in a more optimistic way; that is, it implies that the patient's "memory slips" are not just a problem but an ability and, further, that one can make some alteration in the problem simply by making a shift in *what* is forgotten.

Pt: Yes [softly].

Th: But, anyway, before all of this—I think the most important thing is to seriously give some time and thought to the potential disadvantages of making this sort of improvement. I'd like to ask you, if we could arrange it in our schedule, might it be possible for you to come back once more somewhere in the next couple of days?

   The therapist is now concluding the session, and he is doing that by again emphasizing the intervention of "dangers of improvement." While he has made a number of intervening moves and tactics throughout the session, he has settled on that as his main strategic thrust, at least for this session. He also gives an assignment that can be done within the restricted time span before the therapist sees the patient again. The possibility of a second visit was not definite at the start of the session; but, in view of the nature of the problem and the assignment, the therapist decides to see him again to check on any possible impact of the session.

Pt: Sure.

Th: All right. I'll have to check and see about that. Either I would check with you if we manage to arrange that, or Dr. Y would call you. Meanwhile, would you take some time—a half hour at the minimum, set it aside, and sit down and think about, and make notes on, any possible disadvantages to getting over this problem that you could think of, and when I say any, I mean to reiterate, don't make them restricted to what seems likely and logical, but even if you think it's something that seems way far out, fine. Because to deliberately attempt to think of the far out will free up, free up your vision and your imagination for anything else. There is a sort of a built-in block there that I tried to describe earlier. So would you do that?

Pt: Of course.

Th: OK. Fine. Then that's really all I've got in mind now, except that I again—I appreciate your coming in, because it's mainly for our benefit.

The therapist concludes with a "one-down" departure. To thank the patient for coming in when all he would have gotten out of it is to help professionals is a "one-up" position for the patient. He is implicitly regarded as a teacher of the very people he has sought out for help; he is doing that as a sacrifice, and he is not being asked to acknowledge that an expert helped him—his dignity is retained.

Second Session

Th: I'd like to say first that I appreciate your taking the trouble to come back, particularly on short notice, and even more because it's going to have to be a rather short get-together for reasons of the way they've got this schedule arranged. They're just sort of fitting this meeting in, but I thought it would be worthwhile to do, particularly because I did want to have a chance to check back with you on the matter that I'd asked you to think about. That is, the potential disadvantages of making a change and improvement.

Here, too, the therapist starts with a one-down stance, accomplished by putting the patient "one-up"—he is thanked for "taking the trouble" to come back. Then the therapist immediately gets to the assignment the patient was given in the last session. As a general rule, when "homework" is given, it is almost always checked on specifically, and usually at the very beginning of the session. We not only want to know what the results of homework are but we also want to convey to the patient that, when assignments are given, we are seriously expecting them to be carried out. Thus, homework is given top priority in the agenda of a session.

Pt: OK. I've thought about it. As a matter of fact, I made a list.
Th: Uh-huh.

Pt: But . . .

Th: Do you have the list with you?

Pt: [Sighs] I confess, no.

Th: OK. But I hope you've got it in mind.

Pt: I do. Would you like me in general to give you—sort of just to go down [laughs], down the list in general, going that way? I had some difficulty fantasizing about disadvantages. I couldn't—in other words—I could get started on nitty gritty details of what would happen were I a good performer.

Th: Uh-huh.

Pt: And I'd see if I'm heading—for example, more students to take, which I don't like.

Th: Uh-huh.

Pt: More bad students. And . . .

Th: Yeah, I imagine they're easier to come by than good students, aren't they?

Pt: Much, yes. So then—I would be in a position once in a while of having to hurt people's feelings, which I really don't like to do, to their face. Of maybe sorting out good students from bad students and telling people that they ought to go back to knitting, or something else, which most of them should do.

Th: Uh-huh.

Pt: [Sighs] For the most part, I looked at myself, and I would have to face my own inadequacies as a performer, and I don't— I don't know really what they are yet. I know what . . .

Th: [Interrupting] That you'd be faced with finding out, and that you wouldn't even know what you . . .

Pt: [Interrupting] Well, I might be surprised. I might be quite surprised . . .

Th: [Interrupting] Yeah, but could it be a matter of getting in touch with what is now unknown?

Pt: Yes.

Th: Uh-huh.

Pt: Could be. Be more likely—probably be facing squarely what is known.

Th: OK.

Pt: Or what I suspect, and that is that my talent is limited, and it may be more limited than I would like to suspect. [Pause] OK. That's somewhat what I've come to in the way of a realistic fantasy. Now I can fantasize extensively about it, but that faces, you know, problems like getting an agent. [Sighs] This kind of thing which we talked about last time.

Th: Uh-huh.

Pt: OK. Well, at any rate, what it made me do [clears throat] . . . I'm playing better, actually. I—I'm—I'm playing better in private than I would have before.

Th: [Made a few surprised "Oh's" during the above.] OK, but that's in private.

When the patient is reporting the change in his playing, the therapist is acknowledging this, but only by inexplicit "Oh's." Explicitly, he raises a reservation—"OK, but that's in private." This extremely brief response on the therapist's part is, in microcosm, a clear illustration of an often-used tactic: to convey optimism on the *implicit* level while underlining that optimism by making a pessimistic statement on an *explicit* level. Such "pessimism" is also consistent with the therapist's previous stance of "go slow."

Pt: That is private.

Th: Uh-huh.

Pt: But—I thought about all the stuff—the other things which we discussed somewhat. Is the—what do I really recognize as the minimal first step in conquering the difficulty, or at least making it livable? And—to an extent I've done that, in that I am playing a little better. I'm a little more relaxed when I play, and I was playing something yesterday, and I think I played it with more enthusiasm than I played since I was sixteen. Which—I didn't quite account for at first.

For the very first time, the patient mentions—"more enthusiasm"—some personal interest in his playing.

Th: Well, I can't account for it either.

Pt: And that was in private.

Th: It sounds nice, and I don't want to take away from the immediate feeling of it, but don't . . .

Pt: OK. So here's what ultimately . . .

Th: . . . attach too much to that . . .

Pt: OK. So when I—when I sort of thought a little bit. But here's what's—what my fantasizing has made me do.

Th: Uh-huh.

Pt: It's made me look at my problem as just—as the self-existence of the other side of the problem. As about the same. Advantages and disadvantages as to its self-existence I have now. Therefore, it's not, you know, Valhalla, that I play and perform well. But then, it seems like such an easy thing to do, if it's not Valhalla, just to perform well. So therefore, what I've actually done is to think of the disadvantages; I've thought all—I had thought of the conquering of the problem as possible. And now I've put myself into a—a realistic position on the other side.

Th: Uh-huh.

Pt: So now, having done that, I know the disadvantages of fantasizing all the good things that come out.

Th: OK. Let me see if I'm picking you up clear. I—I get it that, in thinking it over in this way, you moved from a picture in which the present situation is potentially very black and conquering your problem is very white, to "Well, there's not that much an opposition, a sharp difference between the two. Each one has some good and bad to it, and therefore it's not that big enormous difference that it was before"?

Pt: Yes.

The patient has enthusiastically elaborated on the improvement he experienced, but the therapist refrains from joining that enthusiasm, at least explicitly. He confirms the improvement but by prefacing it with "Let me see if I'm picking you up clear," he avoids the invitation to say "That's great!"; moving only to "It now seems no big difference, one way or the other?" Since the therapist had taken a "pessimistic" stance—at least on the overt level—and that stance has aided in producing a beneficial change, he is not going to depart from that stance to the very end of the transactions with the patient: "You don't change a winning game."

Several years after this interview, some informal follow-up information was obtained from the therapist whom the patient had been seeing at the time of the demonstration interviews: Without formal termination, the violinist had gradually ceased treatment; had gone into one aspect of the real estate business in partnership with his landlord; had become successful in this business; and had given up his professional career in music but was continuing to play for his own enjoyment.

❧ 11 ❧

Case Study
The Stroke Victim's Family

The identified patient in this case was a man of fifty-eight who had suffered two strokes, about six months apart. The second stroke had occurred about six months prior to our initial contact with the case. The patient had partially recovered from the effects of his strokes, and both his internist and his neurologist believed further recovery would be promoted by a reasonable amount of physical activity. However, the patient was "noncompliant"; that is, he was resisting the urgings of both his doctors and the members of his family to get on with such a program. Instead, he spent most of his time either in bed or passively watching television from an easy chair.

In these circumstances, Eldon Evans, a member of the Brief Therapy Center who is both an internist and a psychiatrist, was approached to conduct an evaluative interview with the patient (H) and the members of his family—his wife (W; fifty-six years old), and their three sons (S_1, S_2, S_3; thirty-three, twenty-nine, and twenty-seven), all of whom were living separately but locally, and remained in contact with their parents.

We present first three excerpts from this evaluative interview by Dr. Evans:

Evaluative Interview

Excerpt 1

Dr: The second question is: "Say what you would most like to change in your family."

S_1:   Do you want to take us in order, or shall we just speak up?

W: Hon, why don't you start?

H: Well, you're not here because of *me*.

W: We're not?

H: No.

W: Who are we here for?

H: Because of *you*. [Laughter]

W: Well, Don [S_2], you start.

S_2:   I would like to see my father get well. That would be nice, because then I'd feel a lot more freedom myself to come and go as I pleased.

S_3:   OK, I would like to see my father well also, so that he could do some of the things he wanted to do and that he could be able to enjoy his life more than he is able to now.

W: And—it goes without saying, I would like to see him like he once was, and able to work in his woodshop in the garage and do things around the house, and ski, and be a normal human being again, with some interest in living—instead of one who just sits on a chair or lays on the bed all day.

S_1:   I agree with the last three statements. I would emphasize also that I would like to see my father have a return to his health before his strokes, where it would give him more mobility and independence, away from the family unit and especially my mother—to be able to do what *he* wanted to do, including go up to the cabin at Squaw Valley and that sort of thing, and while I don't think it's really responsive to the question, I would say that I'm optimistic that these things could happen, and could begin to happen because I feel that he is improving.

W:　All right, Hon.

S₂:　What about you?

W:　What would you like to see changed . . .

H:　Well . . .

W:　. . . besides *me*?

H:　Well, the thing that bothers me is my mobility, my stiffness, and so forth, which is more of a medical problem than it is psychological. If this leg here had the lift and motion that the other one had, I could—I could run, even. Right now I can hardly walk. And if—it doesn't actually—well, sometimes I can walk all right; most of the time I can't—can't even lift that leg up.

　　Excerpt 2

S₁:　You got to work harder if you want to improve your physical well-being, and I think that . . .

S₂:　Only in improving your physical well-being are you going to improve your mental, and I think that you can do it. I don't know what it feels like to feel what you have in your hands and in your leg.

S₁:　Well, you know—and about that, I realize that I don't have the physical limitations that you do, but you look at television and you see people who are painting oil paintings with the paintbrush held in their teeth, and you may not be able to do the real detailed craftsmanship that you used to be able to do working with your shop out in the garage, but I really think that if you wanted to, you could do a heck of a lot of things right now. I think that it's a matter of saying, "Damn it, I'm going to do this for myself because I want to do it."

Excerpt 3

H: Well, it started out—the question being *me* and the troubles that *I* was having with everybody and everything. I still think that there's a hell of a lot wrong with me physically that the family doesn't give me credit for—doesn't realize . . .

W: You're looking at me.

H: Oh, I'm—I mean you.

W: Well . . .

H: It seems to me that everybody—the way I walk . . .

W: Well . . .

H: I don't walk and drag my leg because it feels good. It feels like hell to drag that fucking leg, and that's no good. I try [crying].

W: Well, when I tell you to lift your leg and stop dragging your foot, Hon, I'm only doing it for your *own* benefit because I think that if you concentrate *hard* enough on lifting that right leg, that you are able physically to do it. It's only been in the last three weeks that you started dragging that foot, and I think it's not only physical, I think it's a little bit of laziness.

H: It is not. It happens. That leg just will not lift.

W: Well, it will lift if you try to make it lift.

H: Walk around behind me and lift the damn thing.

W: Well, we'll get you some lighter-weight shoes, then. Those weigh a ton.

These excerpts indicate plainly that the family members—the wife primarily, and the sons secondarily—are taking the position that the patient's problem is largely a mental one: He is not making the effort needed to be more active; not trying hard enough. The patient, meanwhile, is equally insistent that the problem is a physical one, a problem of inability. He responds to their urging with a mixture of irritation and depression.

This problem was then referred to the Brief Therapy Center. Since the patient was obviously opposed to any "psychological" approach to his situation, and since we believe that an interactional approach offers the possibility of changing the behavior of other members, we chose not to see the identified patient at all but instead to work with the other family members concerned with the problem, especially the wife. Paul Watzlawick was the primary therapist in this case.

Session 1

At this session, the wife and the three sons were present.

Excerpt 1

Th: Well, I guess I should begin with you now as to how you see the problem.

W: Well, in answer to a question that Dr. Evans asked, I couldn't get myself together at the time to answer it, so I went home that night while it was on my mind and I wrote a letter in answer to the question: "How has the stroke affected me?" And I think that will cover everything. I will read you the letter, if you want to take the time.

Th: Yes.

W: [Reading] "For the first six or nine months I spent most of my time holding Sam in my arms, comforting him and crying with him, as well as for him. I guess I cried more than the average person does in a lifetime. His deep depression had such a hold on us both that nothing helped to ease the pain. During these months, I took Sam to the Lakes Medical Center three times a week for speech and physical therapy. I helped him with his homework in speech therapy, and we used a tape recorder to repeat sentences and read and relearn to pronounce words. We also worked on the physical therapy as much as he could be persuaded. He had no interest in this, and so I gave him repeated pep talks and assured him we were going to lick this awful thing that had ruined our lives and he would be the man he once was again. We walked, and I encouraged him; but most of the hours of the day, he spent either in a chair watching TV or sleeping on the bed. In a few short hours, my husband went from a healthy,

strong, intelligent, and capable man to a confused and physically spent human being. I hadn't kept the finances or taken care
of taxes and so forth for years, but I was abruptly plunged into
all these chores again. I spent hours doing book work, as well as
figuring out a maze of hospitalization forms and insurance
forms, and so forth, as well as making all the necessary and required arrangements for his disability retirement. I live in a
vacuum. There is total silence. He sometimes speaks six words
or even may say a sentence now and then. I am criticized for
playing the TV during dinner, but it is either TV or silence. Our
friends have stopped dropping by, and even his friends don't
come over anymore, as it turns into an embarrassing emptiness
when he says nothing, and I am left to try to carry on a conversation with everyone. For this, my sons say I talk too much."

The wife's letter clearly indicates that her position is one
of "helper" to her husband in his difficulty and that this help
has consisted, on the one hand, of doing things for him and, on
the other, of urging him to get on with rehabilitative tasks.
There are also indications here (confirmed by the evaluative
interview) that she is fed up—frustrated and angry about the
husband's inaction in the face of her helping efforts.

Excerpt 2
W: For instance, at Christmas the company gave him a retirement party, and they called him up in front of 150 people to
the microphone. He spoke without any hesitation, he didn't
slur his words, and he made a little speech, and then he was all
over the place, shaking hands with people, and he almost acted
like his old self again.

This report indicates that the patient can function better,
at least at some times and in some circumstances; the disabilities
he has emphasized are not invariable.

Excerpt 3
Th: If we meet here, it would be for the purpose of finding
out how you, being closest to him, can be of the greatest help

to him. You all have already mentioned ways you have been trying to help him, especially you [wife]. You first tried to be very supportive, and then you felt that maybe you shouldn't be, and you changed your approach to him. So as I say, if anything comes from these sessions here, from these few sessions here, it should be, and let's hope that it will be, in the area of dealing with him—helping him in a way that maybe hasn't been tried yet.

The therapist, while carefully avoiding overt optimism, defines the nature of the work. Any success will depend on their helping the patient—utilizing their position as helpers—but in a new way.

Session 2

The wife and two of the sons attended this session.

Excerpt 4

Th: What would be nice is to bring about a change in his attitude . . .

W: Yes . . .

Th: . . . so that he would then begin to do things that he is not doing now, necessary things, everyday, routine things that he is not doing now. How would you most clearly notice that his attitude has changed? What would he start doing all by himself of those everyday, obvious, personal actions that one takes dozens of times in the course of a day that he now is not taking? [Three people talk at once.]

S₁: . . . that would signal to us in an objective way—that would be a sign that he is now doing something that he used to do, and this means that it's progress toward his previous mental state?

Th: Correct—that his attitude has changed, and here is evidence. Yes?

The wife has made it clear in the initial interview, and in

the evaluative interview (for instance, in her references to "laziness" and "trying") that she feels her husband does not have the right attitude toward his difficulties. The therapist affirms this view, then uses it as a stepping stone to move to the question of behavioral change: What would indicate the desired change in attitude? He gets an immediate affirmation of this tack from one of the sons. The sons, somewhat less closely involved, are more responsive to new views than the wife, but correspondingly less crucial for influencing change in the identified patient.

W: Well now, one thing—I make the coffee in the afternoon around four o'clock, because that's when I'm ready for a cup of coffee, and when I pour myself a cup of coffee, he's always in the family room watching TV, and I always pour a cup of coffee and take it to him. So I got so aggravated one day because there was something that I was doing that he could have helped me do and he didn't offer, and he wouldn't help me. So I said to myself: "I have taken you the last cup of coffee. Now if you want a cup of coffee, you will come in the kitchen and get it." So I told him that. So he has since then been coming in and getting his own cup of coffee.

S_1: I don't think that's the response to what . . .

Th: Well, yes and no, because what I'm wondering is what would have happened if you hadn't said anything, but you wouldn't have brought him the cup of coffee?

The wife responds also, but less clearly than the son. She offers an example of unusual active behavior by her husband. Her son starts to disqualify this as not pertinent, but he is checked by the therapist—even a partial acquiescence from the wife is worth accepting and building on further if possible.

W: He wouldn't have come for it.

Th: He would not have.

S_1: You mean he would have done without, even though he knew you made it?

W: Yes, he would have done without until dinner.

S₁: You're sure—and he wouldn't have said, "Would you bring me a cup of coffee?"

W: No, he wouldn't have said anything, and he wouldn't have come for it. Now last night . . .

S₁: Why not? Wouldn't he have wondered: "Look, I always get coffee when the coffee is made"?

W: No, he wouldn't even have thought about it. Now, last night after dinner, when we always have a second cup of coffee, he actually got up and went and got it, instead of asking me for it like he usually does, which surprised me.

S₁: Well, is that not a very small, small scale of what you were . . .

Th: Before we get out of this. What accounts for his getting up and getting his own second cup of coffee?

W: Last night? I have no idea.

Th: He must have felt something *was* different.

W: I probably bitched at him all day.

Th: I'm not sure. I mean, it's something that you must have done or not done at that moment . . .

W: Well, he knew that I . . .

Th: . . . to change his attitude, to get up and get his own coffee.

W: Well, he knew that I was tired. I had been working all day, and when it was time to fix dinner at six o'clock, I said, "I'm very tired and I don't feel like fixing a big meal tonight," and I said, "What kind of sandwich do you want?" So he knew I was tired because I *never* give him a sandwich for dinner. I always fix him a full, complete meal. So maybe that was the reason he got up—because he knew I was tired and he went and got the coffee instead of asking me to get up.

S₁: He might be concerned about your health too. Mom passed out on Saturday or something like that.

The therapist emphasizes that the husband's action, getting his own coffee, was unusual and, presenting the assumption that this *must* have been a response to some different behavior by the wife, presses the question: *What* was it that you did differently? He finally gets some response to this persistent inquiry. The wife acknowledges that she was tired and openly expressed certain limits on her ability to take care of her husband.

The son then joins her in this theme of "incapacity" and the husband's possible reaction to it, mentioning that on a previous day his mother had passed out; she had taken some medication in error and reacted by fainting. This occurrence and the patient's response to it is pursued in the next excerpt.

Excerpt 5

W: Believe me, I'll *never* take one of those things again. I didn't even know how strong it was, or what it was to begin with. You shouldn't give me something like that!

Th: But take the unexpected result of this. Well, you can say it does or it doesn't have a connection with it. To my mind, it has had the unexpected result of having your husband get up in the evening after dinner and getting himself his own second cup of coffee.

W: Yes, maybe that did have some effect on him—the fact that he knew that . . .

S_1:   Don said he came in this morning and sat down on the side of the bed and talked to you because you were dead tired.

W: Yes. I was resting on the bed this morning before I took my shower and dressed, and he came in and sat on the end of the bed and talked to me, which is unusual. He doesn't usually do that.

S_1:   The neighbor called me at the office and I called home and spoke with my father. The neighbor was very concerned over the symptoms she had seen and did indicate that Don was on his way, which would . . . I think that was something that you had indicated a while before, she hadn't talked to you, but anyway, I talked to my dad.

W: I told Carol [the neighbor] that Don was on his way and I would be all right.

S_1: Well, I talked to my father about it, and I said, "Well, what does it look like? It doesn't look like she had a stroke," and I knew the thing which had precipitated all this concern was that the income tax returns were completed and the amount of additional tax due was considerably more than had been anticipated, and it caused a lot of alarm, and still does. Now, my father was very lucid, very calm, and I said, "Well, you don't think that she had a stroke, do you?" And he said, "No. She'll be OK." So anyway, I thought that his reaction was very appropriate.

In brief, this account of the wife's reaction to taking the inappropriate medication confirms the coffee incident. When she appeared helpless, the patient responded actively and appropriately. This implies that any useful change in her behavior will be in the direction of "helplessness"—a move away from her previous one-up caretaking and exhorting position.

Excerpt 6

Th: Let me now—since I have a certain idea now of what perhaps a very small step or two steps may be, let me mention something else that is of, I think, great importance. I've had a chance to watch the videotape that was made of the four of you over at the university, and there was something rather amazing that took place in that interaction. In fact, it took place eleven times in the less than an hour that you were interviewed. Does anybody have an idea what happened eleven times?

S_1: I could suggest—I could say that possibly eleven times he started to say something and one of the four of us finished his statement for him or supplied him with a word.

S_2: We prompted him, probably.

Th: That is also true but is not what I had in mind just now.

S_1: Interrupted?

Th: No, no.

S_2: What—with him breaking down and starting to cry?

Th: I think that was just once or twice.

S_2: Once or twice.

S₁: Let me make this point, too. I think that, for your information, he was—he appeared—his emotions were really on the surface, and he was in much more of an unsettled state on that occasion, with the camera there, and all of us there, and this kind of a formalized setting, than he normally is.

Th: Still, I think this is probably a pattern of interaction that takes place anyway.

W: Well, then, could it have been his rubbing his hands together?

Th: No, no.

S₂: In interaction between us as a group?

Th: Yes.

W: I can't imagine what it was.

Th: The little incidents that I have counted have all the same structure, and I'll tell you what it is. Every single time that one of you, or all of you, were beginning to say, "You can do it," "You can improve if you will only do such and such," "If you will only stop doing nothing, if you get going, you will find that things improve"—this happened many times, but eleven times out of these many times, he reacted. And how do you think he reacted?

S₁: Turned away from the speaker.

Th: That, but there was more to it.

S₁: Did he make a statement?

Th: Oh, yes. Very specific.

S₂: We don't know.

Th: His reaction—it became predictable after it had been repeated three or four times. I just knew it was going to happen five, six . . .

W: Not the hand thing?

Th: No, no. In a more general way.

W: He probably just said, "I can't."

Th: That's it exactly. And I was struck because I saw the four of you struggle very hard to build him up, give him a measure of self-confidence, to point out to him that things need not go on the way they are going just now, that things can improve— and, predictably, every single time, he would turn around and say, "You don't understand."

W: Yes. "I can't do it."

Th: "You don't know what it feels like to have bad legs. You don't know what it means to have one's hand feel the way my hand feels," so that the outsider who watches this tape gets the impression that here are four people who are trying very, very hard and very honestly to bring about a positive change and, as if by negative magic, it has the exact opposite result. What you want to achieve, you not only don't achieve but you achieve the opposite: you bring him to insist even more on the fact he cannot do it, that he is feeling very badly, that you—all four of you —don't understand. It prompts him—of course, I assume, I can't read his mind—but it prompts him to give you more evidence, more proof, of his inability . . .

Referring back to the evaluative interview, the therapist states that a clear, definite pattern of action by the family members and reaction by the patient was visible to his objective and expert eye; it happened eleven times. What was it? As they attempt to answer this question, they become increasingly involved, until they hang upon the therapist's answer. Finally, the wife gets close enough: "When we urge action, he says, 'I can't do it.' " The therapist affirms this answer and builds on it. He gives their good intentions full credit but equally points out that, "as if by negative magic," their actions are counterproductive. There is no blame; only a strange and unfortunate reaction to their efforts.

S_2:   When I was working on a fence this week, I said—the first thing I said—was I got fed up and I just started ignoring him. When he came out into the yard when I was out there, I didn't turn to him and say anything. I just was ignoring him, doing my work; he was standing around giving suggestions, and this and that on the fence building, and he was an accomplished carpenter—he knows what he's talking about—and he still knows. But

he was pointing out—I'm working at one end of the fence and
he's pointing out these boards down here that need work, and
he says: "Now you go get a hatchet and go get a prybar and do
this," and I said, "Look, I'm working down here. You want to
do it, then go do it, but I'll worry about that when I get there."
He went and got the hatchet, he got the prybar, and he showed
me—he started prying these boards up, saying, "Now do this.
This is what you've got to do, and then do this at the bottom,"
which is what I did ultimately, and I would have done ultimately—I would have arrived at it myself. But I was putting in
posts to support the fence and then I was going to worry about
the rest of it later. He was concerned about the immediate problem of the slats falling out of the fence, not the fact that the
fence was falling down in total. So I just said, "Well, do what
you want to do but I got boards going on down here." I ignored
him, and he went and got the hatchet, and he got the prybar,
and he got it and he whacked it into the bottom of the board
and he lifted the board, pried it up, and said, "Now put a nail in
through the top," and I said, "The top nail is not going to do
any good, but we'll do that later. But let me get the fence so
that it's not going to fall over first." But the thing is that he
went and he got it; he brought it out to show me what he meant
because he couldn't explain it. So this is the exact opposite of
what we were doing there. I was ignoring him instead of saying,
"Well, how should I do it?" and he went and got it and showed
me. And he called me a smart aleck and almost hit me a couple
of times.

One son indicates that he has heard and agrees with the
therapist's message by offering an implicitly confirming anec-
dote: When he went about a household job his own way, without actively attempting to involve his father, father volunteered
advice and participation.

Excerpt 7
Th: I think the main burden of making a sacrifice falls upon
you [wife], whether you like it or not, because, you see, so far
you have tried to do the commonsense thing—the loving, reason-

able, logical thing. What could be more loving and reasonable and logical than to encourage your husband to go out and do something to break through this barrier of his inabilities, or presumed incapacities that may not be all that bad, judging from what the neurologist said. I think it will be almost impossible for you to make a switch and say, "I have so far tried to do things in a pleasant way. It may be necessary for me to bring an even greater sacrifice than ever before and adopt an attitude that goes totally against my grain, that goes totally against reason," and, as I say, I'm not very optimistic about this possibility.

S_1: As you describe that second possibility, you're saying that my mother's having taken the one course of action, the loving approach . . .

Th: The loving approach or the optimistic, the cheering-up type of approach.

S_1: . . . that the other approach, the opposite approach, would be what? To let him alone?

Th: Not only that . . .

S_1: To be antagonistic?

Th: Everyone has to go beyond even that. Those are two marvelous examples that you gave me. I couldn't have thought of anything better. You [wife], by sheer mistake, got yourself into a very brief state of incapacity yourself. And instead of panicking and thinking the world was coming to an end, he suddenly begins to function in a way that surprises you by its purposefulness, its reasonableness, by its appropriateness. You [son] are building a fence, and he decides he wanted it here—you are over there—and you take a stand that is different, as you pointed out to me, that is different from what you would have done a few days ago. You said, "OK, never mind. I'll do it my way here," thereby forcing him into getting those tools and starting correcting on it, making it all right over here. That's the thing I'm talking about. That's the attitude that probably is going to bring about a change.

Having laid the groundwork by his "documentation" of

how "You can do it" produces results contrary to those desired, the therapist begins the major intervention of suggesting that a very different approach may be needed to help the patient. In order to promote acceptance of such a change, he defines it not as simple and easy but as a very difficult step and requiring even greater sacrifice—to connect with the wife's position of helping and trying hard. Also, he avoids getting specific about what changes he is proposing. Initially he makes only a general statement. Then when one son, again leading the way, asks what the opposite approach would be, the therapist points out that they themselves have already demonstrated what works.

Excerpt 8

W: You know, he takes care of his own personal needs on his own, like getting up and brushing his teeth, and putting his clothes on. He would sleep in the morning as late as I'd let him sleep, but I get up early and I serve breakfast at 8:00, and so I go in and say, "Breakfast is on the table, so get out of bed."

Th: Does he?

W: So he gets up and brushes his teeth and puts his clothes on and comes . . .

Th: All right. Could you forget tomorrow?

W: To call him?

Th: Yes.

W: OK, I will. I'll just put it on the table and let it get cold.

Th: And what will you do if he says, "Why didn't you call me?"

W: I'll say, "You know what time breakfast is served and you should have been here."

Th: I was afraid that you might do that. Yes.

W: [Laughing] What should I do?

S_1: Say you forgot.

W: I forgot to call him?

S_2: "I got engrossed in the talk show."

Th: Say you are terribly sorry. "I don't know how it happened. I just forgot to call you." Say "I don't know how it happened. I'm sorry."

S_1:   Are you saying to actually prepare bacon and eggs and put it on his place at the table and let it sit there until he gets up at 11:00 or something?

Th: Perhaps.

S_2:   Wait and see. Let's see what time he gets up.

S_1:   He might think that she for some reason decided to cut him off without breakfast.

Th: No, no, no. It should be there. It should be there, and you are simply sorry—you forgot.

S_1:   Why can't she simply say when she gets up and goes out into the kitchen, "Well, breakfast will be ready in five minutes"?

Th: Yes, because we assume that he knows anyway; it's a routine that has been a years-long routine.

W: He knows, when I leave the bedroom, he knows that I'm going in the kitchen to prepare breakfast and it will be ready within ten minutes at least.

S_1:   Ten minutes later it'll be there.

W: It'll be on the table.

Th: So this time you forget, and half an hour later, when the eggs and the bacon are cold, you can then be very apologetic and tell him, "I don't know how it happened, but I forgot to call you."

S_2:   Should she wait and let it sit there?

S_1:   Let's make cereal. [Laughter]

W: I just forgot.

Th: Yes.

S_2:   Well, let me tell you, that'll shake him up.

The wife describes the household breakfast routine, and the therapist proposes that she "forget" to call her husband for breakfast. That is, here is an opportunity, in a limited everyday situation, to begin making a shift from "taking care of him," which involves telling him to get up, to leaving action up to him and if need be, explaining this on the basis of *her* error or incapacity.

Th: It is just as possible that you might say you didn't feel well. But I'm just wondering, indirectly, as are my colleagues, are we being too—are we being carried away by therapeutic enthusiasm? Are we demanding something that is so contrary to your outlook on how to help your poor husband that you will listen to us here but by the time that you walk out of this building . . .

W: No, I . . .

Th: . . . your minds would have changed.

W: No, listen, I would be delighted to try anything you suggest.

Th: Well, I've heard this too often. "Doctor, anything you say" . . .

W: I mean it.

Th: . . . except the one thing we do say.

W: No, I mean it. Anything you tell me that has the slightest, remotest possibility of snapping him out of this . . .

Th: Think, for a moment, how difficult this is going to be for you.

The wife has agreed to follow the suggestion of "forgetting" to call her husband, but the therapist reinforces her motivation by suggesting she may fail to carry out this difficult task in practice. As a dedicated helper, she responds by insisting she will do it.

Excerpt 9

S₁: So what you're saying is that the next morning he'll be out of bed on time.

Th: No, I'm not saying that. We would like to find out what happens.

S_1:   Well, then, should she follow it up the next morning by forgetting—doing the same thing?

Th: I don't think we can repeat the breakfast thing every morning. That would be a bit suspicious. But what about the dinner? There must be other similar small things. Suppose for a moment that you said, "Sam, there's one thing that men usually don't realize, and it sounds silly, it sounds insignificant and trivial, but it is terribly difficult for a woman to dream up a new menu every evening. I just don't know what to make. For heaven's sake, tell me." Again, you will be playing helpless, again you will be doing the very opposite. "Sam, it would be good for you if you decided what you want for dinner." No, that's not what you want to say from now on, but from now on what you will say is, "One of the things that I find increasingly difficult is to dream up a menu, to dream up a dinner."

S_1:   What you have actually said, by the way.

Th: Yes, but do it again in a framework of "I don't know; I can't think; I am at the end of my rope." Do you understand? There's a great deal of difference between doing it in an educational manner where he smells a rat and says, "Well, that's another one of those attempts to get me going and they don't realize how badly off I am." No, no, no! You happen to be worse off, as it were. So you can't think of what to prepare for dinner tomorrow night. "Tell me." And if he doesn't tell you, you then make something which you know that he just detests.

W: Liver [amid much laughter]. That's what caused it last night.

Th: And then, "Well you didn't tell me what you wanted. Here is liver." Oh, no! What you then say is, "Oh, I'm sorry."

Since the assignment has been accepted, and the clients inquire "And then what?" the therapist proposes a further, but similar, task.

Session 3

The sons were unable to attend, so the wife was seen alone in this session.

Excerpt 10

Th: Tell me—how did it go?

W: Well, things have been about the same. I did what you suggested about putting the meal on the table and just not calling him, and it must have sat there I guess forty-five minutes, and then he came out and he really didn't have any response to make, and this is the trouble—nothing bothers him.

Th: Well, what happened next morning?

W: Well, now, every other morning, which is unusual, he got up. I guess the dog woke him up, so he got up and he was on time for breakfast.

The therapist inquires about the assignment. The wife replies that she did it but that "Things have been about the same." The therapist, however, knows from experience that general answers may be misleading or inaccurate, so he inquires further and finds out that the patient's behavior has in fact changed markedly. The wife still tries to explain this as caused by the dog, not by her influencing her husband's behavior, but a step has been made.

Excerpt 11

Th: But let me go back to the other thing then. What about the dinner? Remember the second agreement that we had, that you would ask him what he wanted specifically for dinner.

W: Well, I got what I knew that he did not like and I served it to him and he did grumble a little bit and said, "You know I don't like this."

Th: Yes, and you said . . .

W: I said, "Oh, I just didn't think about it when I was shopping. You know, it's really hard to plan a different meal every night. It just didn't cross my mind while I was shopping, and so you just have to eat what I serve you," because I fix a big dinner for him every night.

Th: Yes. Did you manage to be somewhat apologetic about this bad mistake that you had made?

W: Yes. I apologized and I said, "I'm sorry and I'll try not to serve you this particular food again, because I know you don't like it," and he just didn't say anything. Now this morning he came out, and when he comes out now here lately, he's been coming over and giving me a kiss on the cheek and saying "Good morning," which is an improvement, because he never used to say good morning or anything; he would just go sit at the table with his newspaper. But this morning he did. He said, "Good morning," and he sat down to the table and started reading the newspaper and he didn't say a word. And finally, I looked at him and I screamed as loud as I could, "Shut up!" just to startle him into realizing that he had not said a word.

Th: Well, don't take it too badly. Nobody's perfect. We all make our mistakes.

The therapist pursues his specific inquiry, asking about the dinner assignment. The wife has done this task also and reports an additional change—her husband now says, "Good morning"—although she does not explicitly connect this to the changes she has initiated.

She also reports a spontaneous change, which though startling is probably also positive: Instead of complaining about her husband's silent immersion in the newspaper, she shouts, "Shut up."

Excerpt 12 (At this point, Mr. Weakland (JW) enters the treatment room for a while.)

JW: What you've been saying about that relates to what I had in mind coming in. You've mentioned a couple of times that your husband doesn't say much, and I'm wondering, taking that into account, how you can tell, really, at all for sure, what the impact of the two things you did last week *is*. Because your husband is the sort of man he is, it would be my estimate that the last thing he would ever do would be to give you any direct acknowledgment that you have influenced him.

W: Uh-huh.

JW: Meanwhile, I think it's quite possible that you . . . The

best way I can put it is you really don't know your own strength
—that you have much more potential for influencing him than
you recognize.

Th: We came to see this very differently, of course.

JW: And the one thing I would be sure of is you will not hear
from your husband, "I got a message from you about breakfast,
and therefore I'm getting up." You would never hear that.

W: No.

Th: That, you can wait until doomsday to hear.

JW: So you can't judge by that.

W: Yeah.

JW: You have to make your decision on the basis of other
sorts of indications.

Th: Mostly, on observations.

W: Well, you know . . .

Weakland is concerned about the wife's denial, or at best
lack of recognition, that her husband is responsive to her behavior. As an intervention to counter or disarm this position,
he proposes that, of course, the last thing the husband would
do would be to *openly* acknowledge that she influences
him.

Th: Where the problem comes in is—all right, what you do
with that situation. And I got, in our first two sessions, especially last week, I got this uncomfortable impression that you
are a little bit overoptimistic as far as the power of simple,
straightforward, reasonable exhortation goes. I think you are
trying to make—and this is going to hurt you probably, hurt
your feelings, but I still think that you are trying to make your
task too easy. It would be beautiful if you could simply sit
down with him, talk reason, and he would say, "I guess you're
right. From now on I'm going to change my daily routines; I
will do this, that, and the other." Wouldn't you dearly hope to
achieve that result? You would, would you not?

W: Yeah.

Th: As John points out, this is very, very unlikely.

W: I know it.

Th: So your help . . .

JW: I hate to mention this, but I get the impression your husband is a rather stubborn man.

W: You hit the nail on the head. His medical doctor asked me one day, he said, "Mrs. N, I have the feeling that Sam has been on the stubborn side all of his life, not only since the stroke. Isn't this true?" I said, "He is without a doubt, and has always been for the thirty-five years that I have been married to him, and five years before that when I went with him, *the* most stubborn person I have ever known."

Th: Oh, so it isn't just brain damage.

W: He is *stubborn.*

JW: Well, the only thing I can think of in relation to that is, I don't know what is possible, how much, but to the extent that anything is possible, it seems to be that you are faced with the task of in *some way*—not necessarily head on—beating his stubbornness for his own good. But even to the extent that you can accomplish that, don't expect to get him to openly acknowledge it, because that is just not in him.

W: No, I don't think he will.

JW: He may come around and give you a kiss, and if you ask him, "What's that for?" he won't say, "Because you've helped me." He may just say, "I just felt like it." [JW leaves.]

Weakland goes on to a more general point, reinforcing the idea that the wife needs to help but that her husband needs a special kind of help. Since he is a stubborn man (a view she strongly agrees with), direct advice is not the way to influence him. The husband's refusal to acknowledge help is used as evidence of his stubbornness and as an indicator that she must help him by influencing him indirectly.

Excerpt 13

W: But it is so difficult. When I remember, you know, the man that he was . . .

Th: Stubborn as he was, huh?

W: As stubborn as he was . . .

Th: Yeah.

W: . . . he was always so ambitious and energetic and capable. And in just a matter of a few short minutes, even, you know, for this to have happened to him. Actually, he was better off in the hospital the first week after the stroke than he is now.

Th: Yeah, because now he's beginning to realize the extent of it, et cetera. But you see, this brings up another point that my colleagues made after our last session, and that is that precisely because your husband appears to be—or is—such a stubborn man, I think it is safe to say that in addition to his stubbornness, he's also a proud man.

W: Uh-huh.

Th: That he probably is very, very depressed, or sad, by the fact that now many things he cannot do, or cannot do as well as he did do them in the past. So that in a way, you know, I think by your helpfulness, by your overt taking care of him, you may quite inadvertently hurt his pride.

W: Uh-huh.

Th: You see it, of course, differently; you see it as a kind, unselfish help that you've giving him. You may therefore be very dismayed to find that you have some kind of a strange opposite result.

W: Uh-huh.

Th: But if you have it, it is bound to be precisely because he is a proud man and he sees it differently.

W: Uh-huh.

Th: He sees it as a rather obvious reminder of his own impairment. And he may resent it.

W: That may be. I hadn't given that a thought.

Th: So, be it this, or be it that, in either case I think it will be necessary for you to rethink the kind of help that you can give him and that he needs from you.

W: Uh-huh.

Th: And to do this, I think you just made an excellent suggestion. Tell him—if he complains about his pain, tell him to go to bed early. "Why don't you go to bed right now," assuming it's about five o'clock.

W: Yeah.

Th: Or, if it is during the day, if he complains, say, "Why don't you go to bed early today?" And then sort of slightly push him a little bit.

W: Uh-huh.

Th: What do you think the outcome might be?

W: Well, it's hard to say. I think that he would probably just go on and take my suggestion and go to bed, and, you know, it . . .

Th: But this would not be the behavior of a stubborn man . . .

W: Well, that's true; he might resist and say, you know . . .

Th: . . . or the behavior of a man who told the physician, "I wish she'd stop pushing me."

W: He might say, "No, I'll wait until after dinner and then I'll go to bed."

The therapist picks up on the "stubborn man" theme, adds the related idea of "proud man," and uses this to reiterate the necessity of different help—instead of pushing her husband toward activity, she should push him to rest more.

Session 4

At this session, only the wife was present.

Excerpt 14

W: Well, anyway, maybe we can carry on and maybe they [sons] can come next week, which will be our last session.

Th: Our last session, yes, so I need from you therefore a very detailed account of the last ten days.

W: Well, to begin with, I did what you suggested about getting up and leaving the dishes after breakfast—left them on the table

—and told him that I had to dash out and run an errand or two. And I came back and the dishes were still there. I didn't say anything; I just went about my household chores. That afternoon after lunch, I told him I had errands to run and I went out and I left the dishes again, and when I came home about 5:00 or 5:30, the dishes had been cleared and he had put them in the dishwasher . . .

Th: Yes.

W: . . . at which I was very surprised, so I thanked him for doing it and told him I'd had a very busy day. Every day since that time, I have gotten up and left the kitchen with the dishes on the table, and he has gotten up and straightened them up, which I thought was very encouraging. I suggested to him one day that he—that I was tired of picking up after him, so he has been clearing up his lunch debris, bringing his things in off the patio, and I feel as though he is better. Now, let me tell you what happened Sunday. I was more enthused than I have been since he's had the stroke. His sister came over and—well, to begin with, at the company, if you make a suggestion to the suggestion committee that is accepted, they reward you with some type of either—it depends on how much money it will save the company. You might get a car, you might get a television set, you might get a Japanese-made radio, but at least you get some recognition. So, when he was working—it's been five years—he made a suggestion that would have saved the company $60,000 in manpower alone [but had never received any reward for this]. And so he got out his tape recorder yesterday to start dictating the letter that he wants to write, and he wants me to type it for him and send it off. So I have been very encouraged about his condition. This week—this particular thing now has gotten him fired up.

The wife reports further progress, now stated in relation to her actions, plus a further spontaneous change: The husband has taken steps to get what is due him from his old employer.

Excerpt 15

W: I do think that he has been better. I followed your suggestions. I haven't called him for breakfast. He's come out late three or four mornings, but he never said anything about the fact that I didn't call him.

Th: What about the dinner?

W: The dinner he complained—he complained about the— "You know I don't like liver."

Th: We discussed that last week already. Did you do anything this week?

W: Yes, I did the same thing this week and he complained again. He's never been a person to complain about anything; any kind of food that I gave him, he would eat it. But since he's been sick, nothing pleases him, especially for lunch. I have a terrible time thinking of something that will satisfy him for lunch. As a matter of fact, I told Dr. _____ I married him for better or worse, but not for lunch. [Laughs]

The wife reports further on pursuing her assigned tasks faithfully, with some positive results.

Session 5

The wife and two sons were present at this session.

Excerpt 16

Th: Can you bring me up to date? This is our last session, you know.

W: Well, I can honestly say that I think he is showing improvement for the first time. He has shown more interest, taken a better outlook on life; he's shown more interest in doing things. I was just telling Jim [S₁] he was working with some of his tools in the garage yesterday, and actually went out and did some watering this morning, and swept off the back walk and things like that, you know, and it has seemed—there has been much more . . .

Excerpt 17

W: . . . that he has, he's been getting up in the morning early. This morning is the first morning he's beat me in the kitchen, but this morning he actually was in the kitchen before I was, which is quite unusual.

S_1:   That's amazing. When was the last time that occurred?

W: I mean—he hasn't done that since before he had the stroke. He's always been an early riser, but since he's been sick, he's been laying in the bed.

S_1:   Is he staying in bed as much as he used to?

W: No. Some days he doesn't even go in for his nap.

Excerpt 18

Th: So what has he been able to do obviously alone? Tell me about it.

W: Well, I had continued your suggestion of—since we came—we and others like us have come to the conclusion that he is a very stubborn person.

Th: And he's not only stubborn, he's also proud.

W: Yes.

Th: And he suffers very much from this fate of . . .

W: Yes, he really does. And I have continued to discourage him. Like I'll say—now, some days he'll feel like he wants to go walk around the block four times and I've been definitely discouraging him.

Th: Why?

S_1:   Is that too much?

W: Because this is the way that Dr. Watzlawick told me to handle it—to say "No, I really think that's too much for you, Sam, and I think you shouldn't do that many times around. It is half a mile each trip, and I think you should come sit down and take it easy for awhile." And this, by discouraging him, actually makes him more determined to do things.

S_1:   It really seems to work that way?

W: Yes.

The wife reports further examples of progress both to the therapist and to her sons. Her explanations to the sons of what she has been doing differently, why, and the positive effects of her actions further solidify her new way of helping her husband.

A follow-up call was made to Mrs. N four months later. She reported that her husband's attitude had continued to improve and his activities to increase but that he had had another stroke about a month after the end of treatment. This third stroke was a severe one, requiring some weeks of hospitalization and leaving him weak and clearly handicapped in speech and movement. Mrs. N stated that she appreciated the period of improvement, and now was simply trying to make things as easy and comfortable for her husband as possible in the circumstances.

Somewhat later, we heard from Mr. N's physician that he had suffered a fourth and final stroke. This is a sad outcome; yet it would have been still worse to have left this couple struggling, one depressed and the other angry but powerless, throughout their last weeks together.

❧ 12 ❧

Psychotherapy—
and Beyond

This book has focused on the clinical practice of psychotherapy—that is, how to deal, by verbal communication, with the kinds of difficulties that are customarily labeled as psychiatric or psychological problems and are customarily encountered by practitioners in these areas or in allied fields such as marriage and family counseling and clinical social work. Since the perceived existence of such problems by clients and by therapists is the foundation and starting point of psychotherapy—for each case and for the whole professional enterprise—we took pains at the outset of this work to characterize what a "problem" means in clinical usage. In our view, a problem (or more accurately, a complaint) regularly involves the following features: (1) A concern by a client about some behavior of himself or of another person with whom he is significantly involved, because the behavior is viewed (2) as significantly deviant from some explicit or implicit norm and (3) as immediately or potentially disturbing or harmful to the behavior or to others, and because (4) efforts have been made to alter this behavior, but they have been unsuccessful. (5) Therefore, the client is seeking professional help.

In direct relation to this view of the nature of problems—and with explicit emphasis that our general statements here and throughout this work are offered only as a useful view, not as the truth or the reality—we have presented a theory of how problems arise and how they persist, generally. For us, although the process is similar, the matter of persistence is paramount. This stance differs markedly from the usual concern to label the particular nature of any problem encountered ("diagnosis") and then to seek its basic origin ("etiology"). Our emphasis on how problems persist is closely related to two aspects of our basic viewpoint: (1) We view problems as essentially behavioral. Therefore, any problem must be continuously or repeatedly performed to exist; a problem consists of something *done,* not something that just *is.* (2) This performance is continuing despite efforts to end it, often including efforts by the performer himself. This is why we see the persistence of a problem as the central issue to understand and deal with, no matter how it began.

Our basic theory about the persistence of problems could hardly be simpler. We have proposed that, except where there are clear and definite organic defects, all behavior, including the kinds of behavior labeled as problems, is primarily shaped and maintained ("reinforced," in a general sense) by other current environing behavior; that is, by here-and-now interaction in significant ongoing relationships. To this point, we are in agreement with the general views of the family therapy movement as it has arisen and developed over the last twenty-five years. We have gone further, however, to propose that the specific locus of problem-maintaining behaviors regularly lies in those very behaviors which the patient and any others concerned are performing in their attempts to control or resolve the problem. That is, we have proposed that the persistence (and, therefore, effectively the existence) of problems is based on a vicious circle of reciprocal reinforcement between the problem behavior on the one hand and the behavior involved in attempted "solutions" on the other.

But why would anyone persist in attempting solutions that do not work and, indeed, often make things progressively worse? Explaining the continuance of unproductive or self-defeating behavior is a crucial issue for all theories of problems, even those in which explicit emphasis is put mainly on matters of origin and etiology. The concept of "mental illness" itself proposes the most common and sweeping answer: People persist in unproductive behaviors because their minds are warped and their thinking illogical. But this is hardly more than the coining of an explanatory term, leaving the postulated mental illness now to be explained.

In contrast, we explain the persistence of unproductive behavior on the basis of a few simple observations involving a minimum of inference and theoretical constructs: (1) From early in life, we all learn culturally standard solutions for culturally defined problems. These standard solutions often work, but sometimes they do not. Since they have been learned largely at an unconscious or an implicit level, to question or alter such solutions is very difficult. (2) When people are in stressful situations, as they are when struggling with problems, their behavior usually becomes *more* constricted and rigid. (3) Contrary to the widespread view that people are illogical, we propose that people are *too* logical; that is, they act logically in terms of basic, unquestioned premises, and when undesired results occur, they employ further logical operations to explain away the discrepancy, rather than revising the premises.

Several aspects of this view may be unpalatable to many people—a skeptical attitude toward truth and reason, a drastic simplification of matters traditionally conceived of as deep and complex human dilemmas, and an ironic view of many well-intended efforts at help. Such a viewpoint has great potential advantages, however, precisely because of its narrower focus. If the therapist's basic task is seen as the effective and efficient resolution of problems, then the view described above redefines this task as much simpler and more limited than it appears when seen through the lenses of more traditional conceptions of psychiatric problems. There are no longer deficits in the patient to repair or compensate for, no longer "unconscious hostility" in concerned others to be brought out and changed, no longer family homeostasis in general or the specific payoff of symptoms in interpersonal power as major obstacles to change. Also, there are no longer a host of separate difficulties, each of which must be dealt with, and no longer a history of traumas whose morbid influences will persist forever unless they are somehow overcome by massive therapeutic efforts. Instead, in our view, there are only vicious circles of problem behavior and inappropriate solutions that perpetuate such behavior in the present. Correspondingly, *any* problem is potentially open to resolution by interdiction of its problem-maintaining solution. Moreover, there is always the possibility that if the problem-maintaining cycle can be interrupted and a more appropriate response to the problem behavior initiated, then a positive or "virtuous" cycle may begin. The therapist may need only to *initiate* positive change, not to remain actively involved until all the original difficulties have been resolved.

To propose this simple model of problems and their resolution, however, is not to claim that its effective application is easy or automatic in actual practice with specific cases. For many reasons, it is not. As we have discussed, clients often present their problems and their attempted solutions in obscure rather than clear ways; they may envision grandiose, unrealizable goals; and they may not only cling to solutions they see as essential but also exert powerful influence on therapists to take similar measures. The existence of such obstacles forms the reason why the great bulk of this work has been devoted to the description of kinds of difficulties that commonly arise in practice and to the suggestion of means to deal with these effectively—first by a step-by-step analysis of such problems as they may arise in the typical course of treatment, and then more synthetically by presenting and commenting on three different cases at some length.

We do not think any further summarizing of what we have said about practice earlier in this work would be useful here, and it might well be harmful; to attempt this would necessarily promote oversimplification. Instead, we would rather re-emphasize that, for effective practice, principles must be adapted so as to apply to the specific features of a particular case and to the particular situations in that case as it progresses. Principles can be stated in general, but practice necessarily is always specific and therefore more variable and less subject to definition in advance. For this reason, even the extensive specific discussions of practice given in this book should not be regarded as final or definitive. We have taken pains to set forth a way of applying our basic principles to practice (including alternative means) that we have found useful from our own experience, and we do not think this distillate from our experience should be departed from casually. Yet other ways of usefully applying these principles to practice must exist, and we look forward to their exploration and development by other therapists.

Finally, we wish to make it clear that we do not see our approach to problems as limited to the conventionally circumscribed area of mental illness. We are concerned with human interactional problems in their widest scope, of which only one subset has been dealt with in this book, those problems ordinarily defined as clinical, psychiatric, or psychological. Our basic concepts are not concerned with specific syndromes or illness or irrational thinking, nor even with the family as such, but are general: they are concerned with how *behavior of any sort* is maintained or altered within *any* system of social interaction. Thus, we view clinical problems mainly as variations of everyday human interactional problems, while recognizing that conventionally they are defined as special problems separate from "normal" human difficulties. Accordingly, we view our approach as applicable to any kind of persistent problem involving human behavior, occurring in any sort or size of social-organizational context—immediately applicable in principle, and potentially applicable in practice.

There are two reasons for making this point here. First, for clinicians it provides an explicit reminder of a matter that, while implicit in almost all the preceding chapters, can hardly be overstressed: We see problems as behavioral, and we do not see the behavior involved in psychiatric problems as basically different from any other kind—it is all just behavior, and all understandable when viewed in an interactional context. This is

in marked contrast with the traditional view of both professionals and laymen reflected in the terminology of mental illness
and pathology vs. normality. The traditional view posits that a
problem is located *within* an individual rather than in interactions between people, that it is the result of some deficit or de-
ficiency, and that it involves thinking and behavior that are different from and beyond ordinary experience and understanding.
We believe that adhering to this traditional separatist view of
problems makes their understanding and treatment more complex, difficult, and uncertain. In fact, this view even functions
to make *ordinary* behavior more difficult to understand, by
characterizing it as individualistic and rational to an unrealistic
degree.

Second, we believe that our general views about problem
formation and problem resolution might usefully be applied to
a variety of nonpsychiatric problems—at least conceptually and,
we would hope, ultimately in practice. For lack of a general
framework, these problems have until now been conceived of as
separate and discrete, and have accordingly been dealt with
piecemeal and often inadequately. As an initial attempt to de-
lineate some of these areas, we will distinguish them as (1) difficult behaviors, (2) somatic clinical problems, and (3) organizational problems. These terms will be defined more fully below.
In addition, some of these nonclinical problems already overlap
or directly affect the working spheres of many therapists or
counselors. For these reasons, without attempting to be exhaus-
tive or detailed, we would like to point out some of these problems and suggest rather generally how our approach might be
pertinent to them. This proposal may well appear to involve an
optimistic extrapolation of our ideas and practices, but we ask
that the reader bear with us and suspend judgment for a time.
After all, the interactional approach to manifestly clinical problems represented a radical view only two decades ago. We believe it has since demonstrated considerable value and power—
not least in promoting a more unified view and treatment of
many problems formerly dealt with as very separate clinical en-
tities. Accordingly, the possible extension of such an approach
to further and wider areas may now be worth considering.

The area here termed difficult behaviors would include all those interactions in which difficult or "unreasonable" behaviors occur—which, while not of a sort or degree to be graced with a psychiatric label, result in serious obstacles to the accomplishment of some mutual task. Although this situation may arise in almost any supposedly cooperative interaction, it is clearest in cases where one participant is formally acknowledged as the expert or helper, and the other as seeking expertise or assistance. For example, a not very pressing social problem of this sort occurs when the client of an attorney actively or passively rejects the very advice he has sought, while continuing to retain that attorney. Another and more serious problem is that commonly referred to as "patient noncompliance," involving the medical patient who fails to follow his doctor's recommendations, to the detriment of his own health. This plainly is a problem that may have grave consequences if the medical context involved is a serious one—for example, patient self-care after a heart attack—and correspondingly there has been considerable concern and writing about noncompliance among physicians. With few exceptions, however, medical approaches to this problem have been restricted by the viewpoint implicit in the very term "noncompliant patient." That is, the problem has been seen as an individual one residing in the patient, not as an interactional problem between physician and patient. Also, the solutions attempted have largely been restricted to direct logical means, such as explanations and urgings about dieting, exercising, and taking medications—with not very favorable results. From our viewpoint, this problem needs to be considered interactionally, with special attention to getting away from means to achieve compliance that already have observably failed. In fact, such an approach to this problem has already been tried on a pilot scale by one of our colleagues (Hoebel, 1976), with encouraging results. The point here, however, is that many such problems may exist—for example, problems involving help to the elderly, public assistance and welfare, and administration of adult and juvenile justice systems—to which our clinical approach might usefully be applied with little modification.

The second category proposed involves certain problems

not usually seen as psychological illness and disease. There is already a large body of work on psychosomatic illness; but, as the term implies, such work primarily has been individually and internally oriented. It has dealt with mind and body rather than behavior, interaction, and body. We believe that an approach explicitly concerned with interaction—and with attempted solutions to problems of disease—might usefully supplement existing work on psychosomatics. Beyond even this, such an approach might contribute to the understanding and treatment of clearly organic diseases. After all, even these occur in some environing context, and at the very least their recognition and handling are greatly influenced by behavioral interactions. This, however, is so important, new, and complex a territory that it can only be identified here as a potential area for future work. (A somewhat more extensive introduction is presented in Weakland, 1977.)

Finally, there is a class of "metaclinical" problems, consisting of difficult behaviors involving wider social systems beyond the family. Such problems are quite common, and because organizational size and power often have a multiplicative effect, their practical consequences may be severe.

Problems in this general class may involve either interaction within a single social organization or interaction between social organizations. For an example of the first kind directly relevant to the clinical work of therapists, we need only recall that many therapists work not in private practice but within a helping agency. Such therapists may find that agency organization or policies can present or exacerbate difficulties in working with clients—especially if the therapist has any new or unusual ideas about what treatment would be appropriate. In such a situation, the therapist is likely to take either the position "Administrator X is just a mean, rigid SOB" or the position "It's the system—just the old army game." Such views are likely to lead either to apathetic frustration or to ineffective argument and protest. While we cannot discuss the handling of such problems specifically here—that would require another book at least—we can suggest that some possibilities for resolution or improvement might appear if the situation were viewed as analogous to the clinical situations discussed throughout this book: that is, as a problem of interaction within a system. This stance leads toward a review of the specifics of the problem and the attempted solutions, and a consideration of possible alternative actions. Such a problem, basically involving an individual feeling "one-down" and powerless in relation to some organization of which he is a member, also may be encountered in ordinary clinical practice with clients having work problems, or even with individuals who see themselves as powerless in relation to "the family."

Almost the converse problem occurs where a manager encounters persisting difficulties obstructing the effective functioning of the organization he supposedly is directing—it's not necessarily so great at the top, either. This situation may arise in any size or type of organization, private or public. An example involving a kind of organizational problem that is increasingly common in recent years may be offered: An upper-echelon manager has some rather clear ideas how his organization or division should function, but feels that to act on these would be to "coerce" his subordinates. He may then adopt a procedure of "participatory decision making"—that is, a procedure in which decisions are presumed to be arrived at by equal discussion and voluntary consensus of the group. Any of several difficulties may arise. Discussions may flounder endlessly from lack of any clear direction, or the subordinates may propose directions running counter to those the manager has in mind. Then he must appear to accept a direction he disagrees with; discount their opinions in hope of eventual agreement—that is, stall; or implement his own decision but claim it represents the group view. Any of these courses will both hamper the work of the organization and create bad feelings among the members. Not always, but quite often, the eventual outcome is to conclude that there has been some "conflict of personalities," and an outside agent is brought in to help everyone examine that presumed conflict, usually in group discussion. In our view, this will probably not help, and may well worsen matters; but the problem would be resolved if the manager could simply be influenced to request compliance with the actions he believes correct, even though his subordinates' views may differ from his own. At a different and higher level of organization, this problem may be seen to parallel the problem of parental leadership—or lack of it—in the family system.

The second broad type of organizational problem involves conflicts of viewpoint and interest between organized groups, which may occur at any level or size of organization. Thus, school counselors may encounter conflicts between family and school, or teachers and counselors, about who is responsible for classroom behavior and how difficult behaviors should be conceived and dealt with. At a next higher level of organizational size, there are often similar conflicts between social agencies involved in the same case—say, between a counseling service and a legal agency such as a child protective service. The typical form this problem takes—quite in parallel to that of parents holding different ideas about a child—is argument over which party is *right* in its view, which usually leads only to recriminations, consequent hardening of positions, and some impasse. Again, we suggest that the possibility of breaking such a deadlock is enhanced if one party can back off from the attempted solution of confronting the other as *wrong,* view the situation as interactional, and seek a new approach. This is not to say that such a step is easy—and as the scale of conflicting systems rises toward the ultimate level of relations between nations, it becomes progressively more difficult for the parties involved to alter a position or to find an effective outside agent to help in doing this. We claim only that in many such situations confrontation clearly does not work but instead maintains or increases the problem, and that our approach might help in devising potentially useful alternatives.

In conclusion, we would like to make it clear that in presenting these rather sweeping views we are not supporting what appears to be a growing movement in recent years to "psychiatrize" all human problems. Basically, our position is quite the opposite: We are looking at human problems in general, including those usually labeled as psychiatric, in terms of ordinary human interaction, and at the ways in which such interaction may work out for the better or for the worse.

⚜ References ⚜

Haley, J. *Uncommon Therapy: The Psychiatric Techniques of Milton H. Erickson, M.D.* New York: Norton, 1973.

Haley, J. *Problem-Solving Therapy: New Strategies for Effective Family Therapy.* San Francisco: Jossey-Bass, 1976.

Haley, J. "Ideas Which Handicap Therapists." In M. M. Berger (Ed.), *Beyond the Double Bind: Communication and Family Systems, Theories, and Techniques with Schizophrenics.* New York: Brunner/Mazel, 1978.

Herr, J. J., and Weakland, J. H. *Counseling Elders and Their Families: Practical Techniques for Applied Gerontology.* New York: Springer, 1979.

Hoebel, F. C. "Brief Family-Interactional Therapy in the Management of Cardiac-Related High-Risk Behaviors." *Journal of Family Practice,* 1976, *3* (6), 613-618.

Maruyama, M. "The Second Cybernetics: Deviation-Amplifying Mutual Causative Processes." *American Scientist,* 1963, *51,* 164-179.

Segal, L. "Focused Problem Resolution." In E. Tolson and W. J. Reid (Eds.), *Models of Family Treatment.* New York: Columbia University Press, 1981.

Segal, L., and Watzlawick, P. "The 'D' Family: A Failure to Assess Customership." In S. B. Coleman (Ed.), *Failures in Family Therapy.* New York: Guilford Publications, in press.

Spiegel, H. "A Single Treatment Method to Stop Smoking Using Ancillary Self-Hypnosis." *International Journal of Clinical and Experimental Hypnosis,* 1970, *18,* 235-250.

Watzlawick, P., Weakland, J. H., and Fisch, R. *Change: Principles of Problem Formation and Problem Resolution.* New York: Norton, 1974.

Weakland, J. H. " 'Family Somatics'—A Neglected Edge." *Family Process,* 1977, *16* (3), 263-272.

Weakland, J. H. "Pursuing the Evident into Schizophrenia and Beyond." In M. M. Berger (Ed.), *Beyond the Double Bind: Communication and Family Systems, Theories, and Techniques with Schizophrenics.* New York: Brunner/Mazel, 1978.

Weakland, J. H., and others. "Brief Therapy: Focused Problem Resolution." *Family Process,* 1974, *13* (2), 141-168.

Wender, P. H. "Vicious and Virtuous Circles: The Role of Deviation Amplifying Feedback in the Origin and Perpetuation of Behavior." *Psychiatry: Journal for the Study of Interpersonal Processes,* 1968, *31* (4), 309-324.

Whitaker, C. "The Hindrance of Theory in Clinical Work." In P. J. Guerin, Jr. (Ed.), *Family Therapy: Theory and Practice.* New York: Gardner Press, 1976.

❧ Index ❧